GOD KNOWS

Michelle Lonsdale

BALBOA.PRESS
A DIVISION OF HAY HOUSE

Copyright © 2024 Michelle Lonsdale.

All rights reserved. No part of this book may be used or reproduced by any means, graphic, electronic, or mechanical, including photocopying, recording, taping or by any information storage retrieval system without the written permission of the author except in the case of brief quotations embodied in critical articles and reviews.

Balboa Press books may be ordered through booksellers or by contacting:

Balboa Press
A Division of Hay House
1663 Liberty Drive
Bloomington, IN 47403
www.balboapress.co.uk
UK TFN: 0800 0148647 (Toll Free inside the UK)
UK Local: (02) 0369 56325 (+44 20 3695 6325 from outside the UK)

Because of the dynamic nature of the Internet, any web addresses or links contained in this book may have changed since publication and may no longer be valid. The views expressed in this work are solely those of the author and do not necessarily reflect the views of the publisher, and the publisher hereby disclaims any responsibility for them.

The author of this book does not dispense medical advice or prescribe the use of any technique as a form of treatment for physical, emotional, or medical problems without the advice of a physician, either directly or indirectly. The intent of the author is only to offer information of a general nature to help you in your quest for emotional and spiritual well-being. In the event you use any of the information in this book for yourself, which is your constitutional right, the author and the publisher assume no responsibility for your actions.

Any people depicted in stock imagery provided by Getty Images are models, and such images are being used for illustrative purposes only.
Certain stock imagery © Getty Images.

Print information available on the last page.

ISBN: 978-1-9822-8912-6 (sc)
ISBN: 978-1-9822-8911-9 (e)

Library of Congress Control Number: 2024919501

Balboa Press rev. date: 09/11/2024

Some names have been changed for privacy purposes.

Contents

My Thank-Yous ix
Introduction xi

It's Not Where You Go; It's Whom You Meet along the Way 1
Abandonment and Attachment Issues 3
Reasons, Seasons, or a Lifetime 4
Growing Up 5
Moving On and Mistakes 12
Codependence at Its Best! 15
Burying My Head in Books 19
Patience 23
Karmic Partners 25
Dark Night of the Soul 28
Twin Flames 30
Controllers and Abusers, Manipulators and Addictions 34
Excuses 36
The Universe Works in Mysterious Ways 38
Forgiveness 40
Chakra System and Meditation 42
Letting Go 46
Narcissistic and Codependent Behaviour 50
Shame and Vulnerability 52
Faith and Manifestation 54
Healing 56
My Journal 58

Afterword 105

My Thank-Yous

I refer to my specific person as my SP.

There have been many reasons, seasons, and lifetime people in my life over the years.

I've been grateful for every experience I've ever had: the painful ones, the loving ones, and the helpful ones in disguise.

Relationships have helped me grow into the person I am today; they have enabled me to gain strength through my weaknesses.

Thank you to David for cocreating our children, and to them for being there while I have been at my lowest. You made me know deep in my heart that I would rise and fly eventually.

Thank you to my specific person (SP) for having been in my life and for being a catalyst towards my growth. I had built a wall around my heart to protect it, and I have learned how to let it down through you. Our journey together has been a roller coaster of both happy and sad moments, sometimes torturous and unbearable; but I have learned forgiveness, and I hope you have too. My love for you never wavered over the years; it was just buried under years of shit, anxiety, lack of self-worth, insecurities, and fear.

Thank you to my parents, whom I chose to be the catalysts of awakening my soul and for my spiritual growth, both of them having generational trauma, leaving someone to gain enough knowledge to break the cycle.

Thank you to my work colleagues; over the years I have learned so many things from each of you. I am thankful for my job in healthcare, which has taught me many lessons I'll never forget.

Thank you to my friends all the way back to school and the friends I've had for a long time; some of the lessons we've learned have been priceless. Pam, you have always been there for me when I have been crazy, and you often keep me grounded; and Ged, thanks for never letting me forget the bizarre and stupid things I've done over the years. Kelly, thank you for always being there and learning and growing with me, telling me I'm wonderful, and making me see my self-worth. Jess, thanks for helping me see things from a different perspective when I needed to. I went from book to book, and I learned a lot in a short space of time.

I am thankful for my relationships with people with narcissistic traits. I forgive you. Not only was I able to look at my own traits, but I was also able to put them right.

I am eternally grateful for meeting each and every one of you special people.

Much love and gratitude. May you all have peace, joy, prosperity, abundance, and love.

Love is all there is!

Introduction

This book was in my head for a while, but I think I somehow knew that if I wrote it too soon, it wouldn't have had the ending it now will. I wondered why I had procrastinated so much, but now I know that I had the knowing, but it wasn't the right time. I knew that there wasn't a part 2 to this story. I know that as I write this page and I am turning fifty next week, I am finally putting the pieces together in this puzzle of my life. I knew I could write it, but I also knew that something was missing. That missing thing, which I have come to realize after almost fifty years is the most important thing you will ever have in your life, is self-worth.

I realized that even in the depths of our despair, there is always something good to see—not that I ever saw this. It wasn't until my mid thirties, after I'd lost my dad to a heart attack when he was sixty-seven, that it was the beginning of the breaking and making of my heart. It took a little longer than I thought, but it's all been an experience.

Some of the greatest songs have been written by people in the depths of their despair and over the years have also been my saviour. Thank you, Annie Lennox, for your songs. "There Must Be an Angel (Playing with My Heart)" was one of the first vinyls I ever bought, around 1984, near the same time I bought Bonnie Tyler's "Total Eclipse of the Heart."

I was grounded a lot of the time as a teenager, so I spent plenty of time in my room listening to these songs, and I'm still listening to them in my room almost forty years later. These days I'm still grounded, but in a more spiritual way—a way I wish I had been shown earlier.

I'm going to write about anxiety, depression, narcissism, codependency, attachment, and abandonment issues, personality disorder traits, unhealthy coping mechanisms, shame and vulnerability, addictions, twin flames, emotional abuse, jealousy, craziness, awakening, guilt, and forgiveness to show how the universe graces us with people to teach us, and gives us signs, synchronicities, and lessons in life which lead to the very thing that will put us right and give us peace in our hearts: self-worth.

We've all read quotes and not really given any thought to the meanings of them. I will be adding quotes along the way.

It's Not Where You Go; It's Whom You Meet along the Way

What you resist persists, what you accept transforms.
—Carl Jung

I was born in the 1970s to parents who were chalk and cheese; Mum was a southerner and Dad was a northerner. They had met while Dad was in the army, and I think he joined the army to run away from whatever demons he had. Dad had lost his own father when he was five; his father was twenty-seven when he was killed after the mine he was working in collapsed. Dad never spoke about it, but I knew he'd seen his body in the coffin in the house after he died. Obviously, this was traumatic. Mum had her own personal issues that I believe caused her own wounding. Nana was a matron, and Grandad was in the army. Nana got tuberculosis and ended up in a sanatorium for a few years, and Mum was sent to boarding school. The dance of the wounded souls had begun.

Codependence: The Dance of Wounded Souls, by Robert Burney, was the first book I read on codependence, and it enabled me to see what was happening during my spiritual awakening.

I was brought up never to cry, to be tough. Later in life, I realized that I had adopted other people's traits and had to overcome them. It was only years later when I realized that emotional unavailability stems from fear—fear of being hurt or sharing oneself with another person, fear of rejection or ridicule or of getting hurt in a relationship. As a teenager, little did I realize how this would affect my own life and relationships; the cycle would repeat itself over and over again. I ended up in relationships with people who were not willing to truly commit to me or be loyal to me, mirroring back to me my own lack of self-worth.

I had become a people pleaser who avoided conflict at all costs. I was, in effect, emotionally unavailable myself. I avoided hard conversations, I put other people's needs above my own, I allowed others to take advantage of me and of my kindness, and I found it very hard to say no. I would do things out of obligation, and this included giving myself away to people, as I thought it was what I had to do to be liked, accepted, wanted, and so on. I stayed in unsatisfying relationships and situations, all the while complaining to my friends and my partner about those relationships and situations. I was passive-aggressive and would let it all get to me before exploding in my own emotional pain and feelings of abandonment.

I was codependent!

We should be more afraid of losing ourselves than we are of losing other people. I had been dancing to others' tunes and keeping other people warm my whole life.

Someone in a family eventually wakes up and sees the dysfunction. He or she needs to break the cycle so the problems aren't passed to the next generations. I have two children of my own in their twenties, and they will adopt some of my traits, even the negative ones. I've beaten myself up over some of my life choices, but my family have the same choices I have now—to accept, forgive, move on, heal, and understand the dynamics. If we just let go and trust, life becomes easier.

I have gone from not believing in God as a teenager to believing in him again to totally believing now. I realized that one has to trust God in order to trust the universe. God helps those who help themselves.

I will show my scars so that others know that they can also heal.

Abandonment and Attachment Issues

Looking back, I can say now that I had abandonment issues for lots of reasons. Dad was in the army, and we moved around a lot. I found myself waiting and waiting for him to come back, I found myself waiting in relationships later in life, as I hadn't recognized and healed that wound. I moved schools nine times in five years, making friends in each new school only to lose them again, over and over. Then, when I was around nine or ten, we moved to an army camp in the South of England. My best friends lived in the same row of houses. When I was about twelve, one moved away, then the other not long after that. We have all since reconnected on Facebook, and we have all obviously coped with being army children differently. Military kids say goodbye quite a lot.

It wasn't just the fact that we lost our friends; our dads were frequently posted away somewhere, leaving us. I can't speak for anyone else, but for me there was always a feeling of abandonment. This became one of my core wounds. I would push people away before they left me. I would also cling to people who did not care about me or want me. I felt unworthy of love and lacked self-love, self-respect, and self-esteem. I thought all men were untrustworthy. I wasn't able to say no. I could never ask anyone for help. I suffered from addictions. These are all traits of abandonment wounding.

Over the years, I found and tried different healing techniques. One of my absolute favourites is emotional freedom techniques (EFT), or tapping. This involves tapping on certain parts of the face, hands, and body while saying statements and positive affirmations. It is energy healing and really is the best.

Reasons, Seasons, or a Lifetime

People come into your life for a reason, a season, or a lifetime. When you figure out which one it is, you will know what to do for each person. We learn to be grateful for everyone coming in or out.

When someone is in your life for a reason, it is usually to show you your inner hidden wounds and traumas or something else you need to know in that moment. The person helps you physically, emotionally, or spiritually. He or she is there for the reason you need him or her to be there. Then the relationship ends. The person might push your buttons, forcing you to set boundaries, but once his or her job is done, the person leaves. Let the person go.

Some people come into your life for a season. They bring you peace or make you laugh. They might teach you to do things you've never done or take you to places you've never been. Then that season ends.

Lifetime relationships teach you lifetime lessons. Accept each lesson, love the person, and put what you have learned to use in all other relationships and areas of your life.

Love is blind. It took me a while to get this. We cling to things as humans that we really should let go of.

People will always be there for a reason; we just have to find it.

Growing Up

*Synchronicity. A meaningful coincidence of
two or more events where something other
than the probability of chance is involved.*
—Carl Jung

As a teenager, I wanted more freedom than I had. I met my first boyfriend when I was fifteen, and I could feel the instant attraction. Somehow, we ended up together. We were together for quite a while before we were intimate. It happened only once, and shortly after that, he didn't want to see me anymore, and I had my first heartbreak. Looking back, I think it was mostly the rejection that hurt, and he started seeing a girl from school I didn't like.

After that, I went on a downward spiral. My self-esteem was low, and I just didn't care. When our self-esteem is low, we end up doing things that hurt us. I didn't care then, but as I got older, this became one of my issues, and I suffered the worst guilt. We become spellbound, doing things just to numb out pain.

I was sixteen now, and I had a new boyfriend. This relationship didn't last long. I found in his possession a lot of expensive-looking items that I suspected were wrongfully acquired. I never mentioned it, but somehow, he must have known that I looked. That night, I escaped through the bathroom window and never saw him again. My mind replayed those fears over the years.

Shortly after this, my nana was burgled in broad daylight. My nana was traumatized by this; it was awful. Was this all my fault? Had I caused all this? I beat myself up over it time and time again. I never said anything.

I had my suspicions, but I buried them and never talked about them again. Looking back, I realize I had no control over any of that.

My mum and I didn't see eye to eye a lot of the time. It was spring, and I was nearly seventeen. In the summer, I met Brenda, who said I could work away with her for the summer if I liked. It was an impulsive decision that I made immediately. I was going. It all happened very quickly. I went home and packed my things, told my mum, and left that evening. My mum was upset, but I just wanted to be free. My life wasn't without its ups and downs, but I was free to do what I wanted. I was freer than I had ever been. During the summer on the weekends, we would go to the coast, and I loved it there. We would spend time in the sea, jumping the waves. Brenda was tall and blonde and had the figure of Marilyn Monroe. She was so strong; I'd seen her lift and carry things, making them look as light as a feather. One night at the fair, I was by the stall where contestants had to shoot cans off a shelf with a rifle. There was a man and a young girl standing there. I'm not sure what was said between these two before this happened, but he didn't aim at the cans; instead, he aimed the rifle right at this girl's temple. I remember being in a blind panic; if he pulled that trigger, she could die. I don't think she even dared to move, and by this time, lots of people were standing around. He eventually removed the gun from her temple and pointed it at her leg. He pulled the trigger and shot her, then casually walked away. The girl was hysterical, with a bleeding hole in her leg. That feeling of helplessness was a wound I needed to heal, yet I didn't realize that until later in life. That feeling of helplessness and fear would play out over and over.

That summer I met Shane. There was no instant attraction, but I ended up in a relationship with him all the same and moved in with him. During my time there, I saw a lot of dysfunctional behaviour, which was my norm now. I saw addictions change people from one day to the next. Addiction does that to people, making them people they're not. It was like a warning, and I didn't know then that I'd also become an addict.

I didn't know why all these wounded and damaged people were in my life, and today I think it's because I was wounded too.

Like attracts like.

It kept happening; it didn't stop there!

I was eighteen now, and one winter evening I was put in a position to make a decision that was for the well-being of one of my parents, which didn't make me feel good. It caused guilt I was to carry for years, along with the other guilt I had already collected.

The silver lining was that my parents had started speaking to each other. There was forgiveness!

Guilt has a way of getting heavier and heavier the more you hold into it. We also get a good dose of it by blaming ourselves for things that were never our fault.

I even felt guilt for telling my driving instructor I didn't want to learn with him any more as he made me feel so uncomfortable with his inappropriate gestures.

I stayed too long, and I think I stayed because I'd made friends and didn't want to leave them. Perhaps I had a feeling of obligation too, if I'm honest. Shane and I had a volatile relationship, and I was emotionally explosive, with traits of borderline personality disorder. I'd left him before, and the second time I left, it was for good.

It was around this time that I saw an old lady get run over, which was to periodically haunt me.

I often wondered why I was having these tough and hard experiences, and it was only in my late forties that I realized the reason.

We teach others how to treat us by the way we treat ourselves. Our rehashing of old stories in our minds just brings us more of the same.

I was now twenty-three, and my dad had moved 365 miles away, back to where he came from, a small pit village up north. He was waiting for a bungalow. I knew where I was going; I was always Daddy's girl. Six weeks later, I left Mum's again and went to live with my dad. I had no friends and no job. I applied for jobs, and my cousin used to meet us for drinks at the club where our dads used to drink. I got a job at a factory, and Dad bought me an old Fiesta to get to work. I moved from one power tool to another. It was there that I met Pam; we worked right opposite each other, and we found out that we lived in the same village. That was over twenty-five years ago, and we are still friends to this day. She said she'd seen me years ago playing in the garden at my grandma's.

She had just gone back to work after having a baby. She had split from her baby's father while pregnant. Pam was strong and took no shit, and little did I know that I had a lot to learn.

I was now in a relationship that ruptured the family a little more.

At the beginning of 1998, Dad received a letter from his estranged daughter who he had never met. Before he met my mum, he had got a girl pregnant. When he found out, he left and went to London to become a postman before joining the army, not taking any responsibility. Jan was born in England and then moved to a different country when she was a child. She had written numerous times over the years. I don't know for sure if Dad ever got to read all of the letters she sent, but I read some of them from her when he died. I found it quite sad.

I found out about Jan when I was fourteen. Dad took me and my brother out to the pub at the weekend when it was his turn to see us. There was a picture of a baby sticking out of his shirt pocket, and I asked him who it was. He told me it was his granddaughter. "What … Wait?" Questions began running through my head. "How? Who? When? Also, why didn't I know about this?" He told me about Jan and how she had just had a baby girl.

Over the years, I had thought about them, but now was the time we could do something about it. I told Dad to write back and arrange to meet. I thought about what it must have been like not knowing where you came from. We spoke to her on the phone and arranged for her to come over in the spring.

I was around three to four months pregnant. Dad had gone to the hospital recently for some investigations and had had an endoscopy that had caused a tear in his oesophagus. He had to stay in hospital, and I was there most nights visiting. He was high on morphine and seeing pink elephants on the ceiling. He was aggressive and told me to fuck off when I said he was seeing things. I cried all the way home.

After a few weeks, Dad was discharged from hospital and was half the man he used to be. He had lost so much weight and looked so frail and drawn. Jan was due to visit, and he was still quite poorly. My uncle and my dad drove down to Heathrow to pick her up.

There were some explosive times as people found out about my pregnancy. Ha ha, welcome to the family.

There it was in its full glory—the whole dysfunction in the family for all to see.

I spent my pregnancy constantly stressed. I had always had anxiety, but this was something else. David worked away all week. He had booked up to go to Tenerife in the summer with the lads, and he'd be away for my birthday.

My baby was due in September, and I decided to go on the train to visit my mother the week before my birthday. My train was booked to come back the day before my birthday. I got on the train, and from the beginning of the journey, I could feel pains in my stomach. They just got worse and worse, and I was sweating and having contractions. The lady sitting opposite me said it could be Braxton Hicks, as my baby was not due for another six weeks. The seven-hour journey was nearly over, and I was nearly home, I was still in agony, not knowing I was in labour. I made it to the station where Dad was picking me up. I got home around 7:00 p.m. Dad had gone to the club for a drink even though I was on all fours saying I did not feel very good. By nine o'clock, I was showing other signs of labour, I rang the hospital, and they told me to come in. Dad came back and took me to the hospital, and my aunty arrived. Dad stayed in the corridor, and at six in the morning on my birthday, I gave birth to a baby boy who was six weeks early, and his dad was still in Tenerife. It was over a week until David found out. He stayed in Tenerife until the end of his holiday. When he did meet his son, he had a broken nose and bruised face from diving in the pool on holiday.

I couldn't forgive him. This unforgiveness went on for years, and I threw it in his face time after time. It tortured me, and I was poisoning myself. We enter our own prison when we don't forgive.

The serenity prayer kept coming to me, and I accepted the things I couldn't change.

Two years later, I gave birth to a baby girl. David and I had bought a house, and things were looking up. We were all amicable, but it didn't stay that way.

We had moved in, and soon things started to get on my nerves. I had interference and things making me feel uneasy.

In hindsight, my own lack of boundaries was evident. There was friction between me and David. I was passive-aggressive, and this tendency would build up astronomically in me before I would explode. We would physically fight instead of talking about our issues.

Communication was never present, and I blamed the other person, but of course it was me too. I'd find myself just sitting, seething, thinking about what I wanted to say in my head, but then if anything did come out, it was passive-aggressive.

I was given a job as a cleaner which I didn't want. I hated cleaning, and I didn't like the organization, but it was there that I met Kelly. She was a receptionist, and we hit it off straight away, and she was to become one of my longstanding friends. There are times when you meet somebody and you just know that she is part of your soul circle—the soul sisters we all have who laugh with us, accept us as we are, and are nonjudgmental.

Kelly was ten years older than I was; she'd married, had two kids, and divorced. Over the years, we were to discover the reasons for our low self-esteem, lack of self-worth, and our tendency to give ourselves away without setting boundaries. And we found the road back to self-love.

We weren't aware of narcissistic traits then. But as time went by, we soon discovered which people in our lives could be described as having narcissistic traits. I think we are blinded by them; we can't see toxicity, then, lo and behold, we get our eyes opened to our own set of toxic dark traits.

My Nana died in July 2001. I was going to the funeral. I drove myself and my dad down. My Nana was the apple of my eye and had always been there for me. I loved her so much. We would sit in her big chair together when I was younger, eating our big bag of pick and mix while watching telly.

I returned to more chaos.

We can hit someone else's triggers without even knowing it.

There was a downhill spiral from then on.

Our fights and rows became worse. We lived next door to a nice couple who I think moved because of our constant arguments. I never let anything go and was like a dog with a bone, and things would escalate quickly, especially with my goading and saying, "Go on then, I dare you."

I had started drinking red wine on an evening—the cheapest and nastiest shit I could get. I was trying to forget how miserable my life had become. It didn't help, and I remember sitting on the back doorstep drunk and on the phone to the Samaritans. Absolute victim mode.

It was time to move on, and I put my name down for a council house. Lots of undesirable things happened during this time, as we were each trying to exert our control. I went back to get some things when he was in, which was obviously a bad idea. He had up the Christmas tree that we'd bought the year before, and I was furious that he was just getting on with his life as if things were normal. I saw red, and even though the Christmas lights were plugged in, I went over to the Christmas tree and grabbed hold of the top of it, as it came in two parts. I walked away with it and said, "I'll be taking my half of the Christmas tree." The lights came unplugged, and the glass baubles went everywhere. I stood on them, smashing them to smithereens, and shouted, "Merry fucking Christmas!"

Moving On and Mistakes

I hadn't really thought about my sexuality for anything more than fleeting moments. I guess 2.4 children is what happens in normal life and in going along with social norms.

I was staying at my Dad's for the time being, and that's where I met my SP. She was younger than I and lived in the same street. I felt as if I knew her even before I met her. We got talking and exchanged numbers. I didn't know then that our journey would last a lifetime. That night, I lay awake all night. It was a Saturday night, and there was a party going on over the street. We got a tent and some cans of lager and spent the night talking. From that moment on, we were inseparable. When the kids were at their dad's, we would go nightclubbing in town. She was more reserved, and I was more the wild type. We would stay at the same hotel at the weekends.

Things started to go south, as we had obstacles.

I guess there's something to say about overcoming obstacles.

On New Year's Eve, we had been out drinking. Around 11:30 p.m., I knew my dad would be back from the club, so I went round to wish him a happy New Year. He asked me about me and my SP, and I denied it. I regret that split-moment decision to not tell the truth. Dad drew back his arm and punched me in the face, breaking my nose. There was blood everywhere—all over my face and hands. I said I would never speak to him again. The next day, I had to get the tweezers to remove a piece of bone that was sticking out of the bridge of my nose. You're not supposed to have regrets, as everything in our life is relevant, but that regret would linger all my life until I healed it.

I did eventually go back home; it was as if it had never happened. We never spoke about it again. That's how I knew he was sorry. I knew, but it was unspoken.

I got a council house. I don't think I was there longer than a year. I still didn't tell my dad. I had done this out of fear. Coming out in those days wasn't as easy as it is now, and I was worried about the kids.

Also, what I learned from the broken nose was that it wasn't safe for me to be who I really was.

We probably should have moved away somewhere together, but was that really the answer?

We both had issues. It was exhausting, the running and chasing.

We both saw other people, but we always gravitated back to each other. The fear of being alone was too great. The feelings of unworthiness were relentless, and I battled with my feelings for my SP and what was good for my kids.

I went back to David. I was still in contact with my SP.

Obviously, I had gone back for the sake of the kids, and I did try to make it work. We went on holiday with David's friends and their kids.

He drove the wrong way around the roundabout where he'd been on holiday while I was pregnant. It was like a red rag to a bull. I had not forgotten and certainly not forgiven.

We went on another holiday with the same people. It was all-inclusive, and the drinking started at around 10:00 a.m. We just didn't get along. One night in the hotel room, we were arguing so loudly that security came and knocked on the door. I couldn't put it right, not with all the best will in the world.

During this time, my kids saw altercations with my dad and other family members. Everything had gone to shit, and there was nothing I could do. There were times I needed someone to have my back, but no one ever did.

I went back to my dad's and put my name down for another council house. There are only so many rock bottoms that you can take before you realize you have to try and sort everything from the bottom up.

By now the only way was up, but that wasn't before I fell back down a good few times.

I was lucky getting a council house right next door to Pam. It only had two bedrooms, but the kids were still young, and they had bunk beds. My SP was back in my life. I was still in denial, and every time things got difficult one of us would do a runner. She went on holiday abroad with her friends. She was on the phone all the time and had been there three days when I told her that if she didn't get a flight home, I never wanted to speak to her again. She rang me back to say she'd booked a flight and was arriving at the airport at 3:00 a.m. I drove down to pick her up.

Codependence at Its Best!

*Experience is the hardest kind of teacher. It gives
you the test first and the lesson afterward.*
—Oscar Wilde

Codependency can occur if you let another person's behaviour affect you and you try to control another's behaviour. We can do this subconsciously.

Eventually my SP and I split up, but I can honestly say there was never a day I didn't think about her. It was a dance of wounded souls. My own insecurities and body shame made me feel a kind of relief that she'd never have to see my insecurities, which were growing exponentially.

Little did I know this wasn't the end to the toxicity in my life.

I missed her, but it was over for now. One night I was sitting bored and decided to join a dating website. I started messaging someone, and I went to meet him. I looked at him and wondered why I was still there talking to him, but I didn't want to be rude and just leave. I guess that's the empath in me, worrying about other people's feelings. Somehow he said all the right things, and I decided to see him again. Only looking back can I see the red flags.

Others will show us who they are; we can ignore the red flags or believe them.

I was a total codependent who probably needed somebody messed up in my life to fix. And messed up this person was.

I was just about to learn some of the biggest lessons in my life.

He admitted he was an addict. With any addict, there is an enabler. We would drink a lot at weekends, and I was enabling his behaviour. Every weekend was a party. Yet I still failed to look at my own issues. I could see them in others and wanted to fix those instead.

We booked a holiday abroad. What I should have done was run away as far as possible, but I didn't. There were lessons to learn!

We were due to go on holiday in the summer, and around four weeks before that I found out he'd cheated again.

By now I had lost the plot with that and everything else.

We decided that we would still go on holiday even though we weren't together. This was probably not the best idea I've ever had, but probably not the worst either.

Fortunately, it was only for a week. I had driven over with my case in the boot of the car, ready to go into the taxi. He told me to bring it in, but I didn't, as I had an uneasy feeling.

We got there, and he was so angry. I later read all about narcissistic traits and how one of the things narcissists do to exert control is totally ruin holidays, birthdays, and any other dates with any significance. We made it to the hotel, and as we were heading to the room, he lifted up the suitcase above his head and threw it right along the corridor. I remember ignoring this and carrying on to the room with my own suitcase. Narcissists don't like to be ignored.

He hardly spoke to me all holiday.

I'd go for breakfast on my own, and he would come and sit on my table, asking me why I hadn't waited for him. We did go to one of the waterfront cafes to see the sunrise, but we didn't stay friends long enough to see it. We argued again. I missed the sunset as I went back to the hotel. I disliked him with a passion.

We got home. I was still alive. We went our separate ways, but my lessons were still not over.

I went out with Kelly a lot, and I went to a party over the road where I and my SP had been years ago. I hoped I would see her and was sitting there when I saw her standing with a group of people. My heart! I got talking to her, and it was like before all over again. My world. She stayed at my house that night. She went home in the morning, and I didn't hear from her again, and I didn't contact her either.

Neither of us was sure why we connected later in life. But I'm guessing that we each had lessons to learn separately.

I was due to go out one Saturday. I woke up that Saturday morning, and it was around 9:00 a.m. when I got a text from my SP telling me there was an ambulance outside my dad's. I never replied to her. I rang Dad's phone number, and it just rang and rang. Eventually the person who took him a newspaper every morning answered. He said my dad was gone; I had already known this in my heart, but the bottom just dropped out of my world, and I fell to my knees on the floor in pain that I can't describe. I felt as if I had gone into a bubble. Throughout the morning, I had to tell everybody. I ran a bath, the only place it was felt safe to cry. I never messaged my SP back. My heart was broken. I guess I had to deal with my own feelings on my own. I've never gone through pain like it, and when I was on the floor, I didn't think I'd ever get up again. All of a sudden, I had so much to do that I could hardly think. I went through the phone book and let people know, having long conversations. I rang Jan, and she said she was coming for the funeral. My mother had never met Jan, but now they were all going to be in the same place at the same time.

It was around this time I started my spiritual awakening, and if I thought it was going to be quick and easy, I had another think coming. It's hard to explain, but I just knew something was guiding me at the time. I felt as though I was having a breakdown and that I was going crazy. After all the narcissistic abuse and angry outbursts and then losing my dad, it was time for my heart to start breaking open. I loved my dad despite his faults. Both my parents had unhealed issues of their own, and he did love my mother. If he was anything like me, he just couldn't show it or never knew how.

I got a job in a GP surgery in 2004 when I moved into the council house. I was in the process of buying it when my dad died, and it was all finalized in early 2007. He left me some money, and I was able to make an extra bedroom in the loft space. I loved my job. It opened my eyes to see that there were so many people with mental health issues, and I wondered why. I was off for four weeks when my dad died, and I didn't really want to go back just yet, but I hadn't been there long, and any more time off would have been unpaid. I was a total mess and never thought I'd recover from the pain. I had lost my Christmas savings when the company went into administration. The kids were six and eight, and I had to do Christmas shopping for them. With the immense emotional pain, I don't know how I got through those months. I was lucky to have Pam living right next door, and I spent Christmas with her and her family. David would come over early in the morning on Christmas to watch them open their presents. It was much better now that we were amicable, and he didn't push my buttons as much.

He got married, and the kids had a stepmum they liked.

Burying My Head in Books

My meltdown went on for months. Each lunchtime, I would go to the library and get out another book I had reserved online. most of them were self-help books. I once got a £25 fine for having eight books out longer than I should have. But every night, I was reading. The librarian asked me what course I was doing after a few weeks, and I said I wasn't doing a course and that they were all for self-help. I'd wondered how and why somebody could be so abusive in a relationship and why someone would tolerate it. Again, I had my eyes wide shut. I came across the word "narcissist" online, and I'd never heard of them at that point, but I began reading everything about them. It became an obsession if I'm honest. I found Sam Vaknin's book online. He's a self-professed narcissist, and his book was all on a blog in those days. Everything began to make sense. Vaknin explained the things narcissists do, the people they target, and all the red flags I ignored. I was just so relieved to have found some kind of explanation.

It takes time to recover from the abuse. Being the mess I was, my doctor had referred me to a psychologist. She asked me what sort of a childhood I thought she'd had, and I said I didn't think she'd had a very good one. She told me that I was wrong and that she'd had a very happy childhood. She also told me that I must stop reading books. I wasn't going to stop reading books; they had been my biggest help. I also got the vibe that she was in denial about her childhood. I knew this was not going to work for me; I wasn't stupid. I also knew that a lot of therapists go into that line of work when they have issues themselves. I knew beyond a shadow of a doubt that this was not for me. I did go for my second session but was told that she had gone on long-term sick leave, and I never saw her again.

I'd read about Stockholm syndrome, which is where a kidnapped person develops feelings of trust and affection towards his or her captor, and that's kind of how I felt, as if I had been groomed or brainwashed. Narcissists do this; they devalue you after the love-bombing stage and putting you on a pedestal. I felt weak, in pain, drained, and as though all my life had been sucked right out of me—all my energy, my life force—and I was running on empty. People who haven't been involved with a narcissist probably would never understand if someone who had been tried to explain the things that happened to him or her. It's so insidious. People would think that the person was crazy. The hundred small things, when added together, make for a very big thing. So many little things make up the larger picture. I feel that only somebody who suffered narcissistic abuse would understand.

Strange things had happened to me over the years. I found glue in the charging port of my son's Game Boy, a broken disc in the PlayStation, punctured tyres, a smashed windscreen, ruined parties, and ruined birthdays, funerals, and Christmas. I had bleach spray squirted in my face and on my clothes and told it was a joke and that I was overreacting; I was told that I was too sensitive and couldn't take a joke. One partner urinated in the wardrobe, so drunk that they thought it was the toilet. I'd been driven round doing donuts in public car parks when another was having a meltdown. I'd been scared witless when someone said that they would set my home on fire; I recall putting water buckets at the door and windows and crawling across the floor while being on the phone to the police. I was dragged through a hotel foyer by my hair. I was controlled by fear. I had CDs smashed that I liked, my phone had been smashed, and I would clean and scrub the house for fear of being told I wasn't good enough. My nose was broken twice, and I suffered black eyes. I had to make trips to A&E. A kettle was thrown at my head, and things were smashed up in front of me. I was coerced into doing things, was gaslighted, was cheated on, had word salad used on me, and was called stupid, and I became a shell of my former self.

I still wanted to fix others and not me.

Narcissists leave others clues. But not wanting to be confrontational, I continued walking on eggshells. Lots of strange things happened during this period, but if I dare to bring these things up, I would get answers like "Why would I do that?" "You're crazy", and "Why are you lying about me?" All this distorted my reality, and over a period of time, I really did feel as if I had gone insane. But I knew this now and was starting to put all the pieces together. The chaos and confusion eventually turned to clarity.

I found that I didn't have to look for the answers; they came to me.

Lao Tzu's quotation "When the student is ready the teacher appears" was definitely true for me. Whenever I needed to know something, somehow the knowledge would appear.

The universe works in mysterious ways.

At desperate times I had said, "God, please help me" or "Why has this happened to me?" but what did I learn from that?

I'd read a lot of books, and one of the first was about dealing with my anger. Then came everything on borderline personality disorder, all the books about narcissists, and everything about codependency, the human psyche, and trauma. I think I read the whole self-help section. I also watched every YouTube video that A. J. Mahari had made on borderline personality disorder.

I'd seen on Facebook that my SP was in a relationship. That hurt and made me sad, but she looked quite happy. I hadn't fixed myself in time for anything, and I felt as if my boat had left the harbour without me.

I was still drinking at weekends and smoking a lot, and I decided to add gambling to my afflictions. At this point, I was a total and utter mess. I don't even know how I got through it. I had a payday loan account, and they'd just let me borrow hundreds of pounds, and it would be in my bank within a couple of minutes. I was so glad when they went into administration and I couldn't use them any more. There were other payday lenders as well, but that was the main one. I got into arrears with my mortgage quite a few times and had to set up repayment plans. One day I got a letter saying that they were thinking of repossessing my home. I managed to pay what I owed, but it wasn't enough to stop me, and this continued for years. The universe must have been on my side somehow. I did try to stop, but nothing worked. The trigger was emotional pain, and I was now a hopeless addict and didn't know how to heal. The more I drank, the more I gambled; but the more drunk I got, the more risk I took. When I risked more, I would win more, but regardless of how much I won, I would often gamble it all away. It was relentless, and my life was overtaken by this.

I had read about the twelve steps for addiction on some of Robert

Burney's pages online and set about doing them, but my heart wasn't in it. I read all about addictions and why we have them, and yes there are triggers, but the conclusion is it all comes down to a lack of self-love.

I had none of that!

I struggled with this right into 2022. As I wrote the original draft of this book, I was 100 per cent sure I would not do it again. That was not the first time I had said this, but it was the first time I cultivated self-love. I did not want to be a menace to my own destiny! Up to 2024, however, I struggled with it repeatedly.

Most spiritual writers I know about have had some kind of addiction or another.

PATIENCE

Patience is a virtue.
—William Langland

My dad always used to say that Rome wasn't built in a day. That was the only piece of good advice he ever gave me. I was always impatient and wanted everything to happen there and then. I've been given lessons in patience many times over; I am hopeful I have learned this one now.

I think my problem was my impatience of not knowing everything right now. I got so frustrated, then eventually I had to switch off and numb the pain and the frustration. The problem with addictions, though, is that they are short-term relief.

I knew there had to be another way, and I did not take this up until a lot later. I'm the kind of person who likes to have all of the pieces of the puzzle before putting them together. Some of the most important things are healthy mechanisms like self-soothing, self-care, and self-love.

Anyone with self-love has a solid foundation. He or she does not have room for self-destruction.

We learn our triggers for our addictive behaviours. I think mine was abandonment, and a lot of times the only one abandoning me was myself. Only when we realize the root cause can we heal it. Other triggers can be guilt, shame, fear, and regret. I had these also. I never knew how to forgive myself, but I always tried to forgive others. Over the years, I thought I had been forgiving, but I would throw things in others' faces if I thought they weren't sorry enough.

Even the feeling of chronic anxiety is an addiction. That feeling in my belly around my sacral chakra and solar plexus chakra felt normal, and I felt strange if it wasn't there.

I had found how to strengthen and balance my chakras online. But at the time, I dismissed them, as it seemed a little woo-woo to me.

These days I realize the importance of the chakra system, including clearing and balancing the chakras. The chakra system are 7 energy centres aligning vertically along the spine.

> I am
> Divine (crown)
> Connected (third eye)
> Expressive (throat)
> Loved (heart)
> Strong (solar plexus)
> Creative (sacral)
> Safe (root)

They make so much sense now. They constitute the whole energy system in the body.

By this time, I'd read a lot of books and watched a lot of YouTube videos on every self-help topic imaginable. I knew the answer was out there somewhere. I knew there had to be a secret to navigating through life.

As John 8:32 states, "The truth will set you free." It was finding that truth that I found so hard.

Now the truth to me is

> Love
> Peace
> Forgiveness

Each of us is a spirit with a human body, having a human experience.

I had almost driven myself crazy looking for the truth, in between drinking, smoking, and gambling. I had found the truth piece by piece.

Karmic Partners

I had learned a lot from my relationships retrospectively, but only now did I realize that there is a purpose to it all and that we get karmic partners as catalysts for growth. They are parts of our soul family who interact with us to show us the lessons we need to learn.

Ego relationships often result in control issues, repeating patterns, selfishness, aggressive behaviour, jealousy, fear of rejection, and a lack of boundaries normally present in a healthy relationship. There are many more examples that are all there to be brought into the light to be healed. Lessons for me had been learned and I had healed a lot.

We can cling onto these relationships out of codependency and low self-esteem, lack of self-worth, and fear of being alone. No relationship with control and fear in it is a healthy relationship. We repeat the same cycle over and over until we learn the lessons; until then, we are just left wondering what went wrong. We can leave that same relationship, but if we haven't learnt the lesson and healed from it, we will repeat it again with a different partner.

Karmic relationships aren't meant to last but to teach us lessons in self-worth.

Nothing quite prepared me for the day that I saw my SP and she told me she was pregnant. It felt as if my heart had been ripped out again. She had got married, and they had gone on to have another baby. I had lost her, and I did nothing but beat myself up about it.

I continued drinking and gambling to numb the pain as a coping mechanism.

An old boyfriend, Ben, came back into my life for some reason. He and his partner had split up. He came to visit, and it was good to see him after all these years. I hadn't seen him for years following a wedding David and I had also attended.

At the wedding, as the celebrants were reading their wedding vows, David had turned to me and said, "I love you." I looked at him and said, "Well, I fucking hate you." Obviously, these days I would never say anything like that, but at the time I could not hold my feelings back, and it did not make for a peaceful or enjoyable day.

The karma of that relationship had run its course. I'd been shown my lack of self-love over and over, yet I still failed to love myself fully.

My life was chaotic. But I eventually learnt some lessons.

I knew that there was a reason for these relationships and the problems that they brought with them. They shone light on the unhealed parts of me, bringing them to the surface to be recognized and healed.

Both twin flames and karmic partner attraction is energetically based. The difference is that karmic partners are based on negative energetic patterns that need bringing to the surface and healing. Once that is done, there is no more attraction to the karmic partner, and he or she will leave your life on that level. With a twin flame, the love never dies.

A karmic partner is perfect for healing unhealed traumas. Many relationships are karmic, including relationships with parents, children, and friends. When I was pregnant, I didn't have the eyes to see it at the time, but my relationships were replicating the unworthiness I had felt in the past. It couldn't have been more evident than with my dad leaving to go to the club when I was in labour, which was how I felt when I was little—as though going to the club was more important than me. In such situations, it's as if others make you feel so unworthy, but you have no other choice than to discover your own self-worth.

The karmic cycle can go on for months or years. You can start families with a karmic partner, but only when you feel so disconnected from your soul—causing you emotional pain, sadness, and hurt—that you wake up to yourself and stop betraying yourself. It's like the tarot card the eight of swords, on which a woman is blindfolded and loosely bound and surrounded by eight swords. She has only to move her arms to be free and remove the blindfold. The card represents being blind to the truth, being in a self-imposed prison with the possibility of new perspectives. You need only remove the blindfold.

Oddly enough, the karmic relationships are blessings, and they have soul contracts to come into our lives and shine the light on our unhealed emotional wounds, and vice versa. I was a karmic partner many a time.

When you are in a relationship with a karmic partner, you will most likely feel energetically drained and end up feeling a huge loss, maybe a huge dent to your confidence and self-worth. You can find yourself pitted against other people, put in competition with them. You weren't being honoured, which makes you disconnected from your energy in this connection, but just remember that this is to teach you the meaning of self-worth and also to learn a lesson in jealousy or whatever negative trait you may have, and to teach you the self-sabotaging patterns within yourself. Just know that this is happening for a reason. You must reclaim your power and work on your self-worth and self-confidence. Your intuition will tell you that you need to walk away from this type of energy and focus on yourself. Only then will you break the karmic contract with the karmic partner. No longer seeking external validation from this person, you will centre yourself in your own self-worth. You must break the cycle. All of a sudden, you will realize how much power you've been giving away, not only to that person but also to lots of people in your circle. Ultimately, you will reach a point where you reclaim your power, which your karmic partner just illuminated. You will be given clarity when it's time to take back your life. Only you hold the key. You will start making empowering choices. No longer will you seek external validation from the arrogant people in your life who make grand promises not backed by action. You will release yourself from the prison of stagnancy and inaction, and no longer will you allow your self-respect to be trampled on. You will have raised your energy and vibration, and life will start to feel better—a whole lot better. (The Hawkins vibrational scale shows how the energies work and you can find examples of the scale on the internet.)

Dark Night of the Soul

At the end of 2017, I had another dark night of the soul. My life seemed such a mess. I had had a few before, but this one seemed particularly hard. I couldn't eat or sleep, the insomnia was the worst I've ever had, and I was grinding my teeth. I would lie in bed crying my eyes out. I'd put on weight; I was so miserable, I think, that I just comfort ate. Everything seemed like a struggle, and I didn't want to get out of bed in the morning and felt I'd be better off dead.

Have faith.

There can be no rebirth without a dark night of the soul, a total annihilation of all that you believed in and thought that you were.

It's ego death and a journey to the light.

This was my second major dark night of the soul. They come at times when you have suffered a major life crisis, such as losing a loved one or experiencing a betrayal. It's more than a depression; it's an existential crisis with doubt and loneliness. Buddhists call it "falling into the pit of the void". I felt I'd been zapped of life. It's a death of the ego, a rebirth. Each time I experienced a dark night of the soul, I felt I came out of it a better person. I had grown. When you emerge from a dark night of the soul, you have a sense that you are changing. It brings the darkness to the forefront, and you come to understand your spiritual lessons.

Meditation quiets the mind, and the relaxation will take the pressure off of trying to figure everything out. The stories and illusions my mind were offering me were making me feel burnt out. I read a sentence that made total sense: "you don't need to 'be more' you need to 'be' more." Just "being" meant getting out of the mind, switching off, and being in the present moment. I didn't really understand why or how to do this until I read *The Power of Now*, by Eckhart Tolle.

God Knows

You become a dragon slayer, facing all your fears and the repressed parts of yourself, your traumas, and your beliefs. You feel your feelings so intensely. You can run from them through your addictions, which is what I did for the most part, or you can stand and fight that dragon with everything you have. Without learning to quiet the mind and just be, without learning to feel wholeness within yourself without attachment and codependency, you will suffer, and the dark night of the soul will creep up on you again and again.

Beyond the fractured mind and with the calmness of mind, you will be able to put together the fragments of yourself and rebuild your life.

It's a journey of struggle and growth and major self-realization.

It's where we learn who we are without people telling us. It is where you feel as though your heart is in mourning, and that is because, deep down, you long to feel the presence of your soul again. You reach a level of wisdom that offers true healing and peace. You'll know at a core level that something is lacking in your life even if you don't know what that is yet.

But it's self-love.

Twin Flames

I was reading all the spiritual stuff mentioned above, and I figured that I was an empath, a star-seed, a lightworker, and a twin flame. I knew very well who I thought my twin flame was.

The ancient philosopher Plato describes the concept of twin flames in his play *Symposium*. Plato writes that the human was split into two halves, one representing the masculine and one the feminine essence, and since then, these two halves have been searching for each other. The so-called twin flames represent the love that is liberated of all conditions.

You and your twin flame may find that you have a lot in common as far as values, past experiences, and interests. The psychologist Spinelli adds that both of you will find that your past story contains a lot of coincidences and similar experiences.

I thought I'd learned plenty of lessons from my karmic relationships, and I had hoped that I had learned enough not to be hurt again. I was wrong. I'd learned some valuable ones, but it was a work in progress.

I thought I knew enough about codependency and that I was no longer codependent. I thought the same about attachment, about control, about trust, and about love.

But my test was on its way.

These relationships push you to grow, a perfect mirror for your wounds. There's a lot of confusion as you try to piece it together.

You enhance each other's evolution and trigger the deepest wounds you never knew existed. After the initial phase of bliss, you go apart to work on the inner healing because it all surfaces in your life at once.

You'll feel as if you're losing your mind at times, as your love for the other person is so deep, yet somehow you know you can't be with him or her, and you feel the most intense pain you've ever felt.

You'll come together and say goodbye again and again. The ego fear comes up, so you run away. If only I had known these were all just lessons to learn.

When I said goodbye to my SP all those years ago, all of the above now made sense. I didn't want to go, but the push-pull dynamic had got old; it was so painful. The higher self knows what you need to learn, and in the grand tapestry that is life, it finds you the perfect person to do that with—be it a karmic soulmate, a family member, or someone else—and it will be for your highest good.

I had hang-ups, I was older, we were the same sex, I had issues with my body, my self-worth and self-esteem were low, and I generally did not like myself. I felt that if I was imperfect in any way, then it was safer to leave no matter how painful. It was just distorted thinking.

There were obstacles that I didn't have the courage to jump over at the time. I lived with regret all those years. But we would split up, we would start seeing other people, and all the ego-based problems got in the way: jealousy, unworthiness, trauma, and arguments.

Love is not enough while the ego is in the way.

The twin flame relationship goal is to experience liberated and unconditional love.

With the ways we acted at times, there was nothing unconditional about it.

Subconsciously I knew I was never going to get married unless it was for true love.

Your twin flame will unconsciously trigger all of your fears and insecurities and will do it over and over again until you know what unconditional love means.

Unconditional love means just that. Your twin flame can run from you numerous times, cause you pain, and give you empty promises, but your heart does not close.

Unconditional love means recognizing the other person's flaws and yet seeing beyond—seeing his or her shortcomings but being able to stay unaffected by anything he or she does. The question is, Will you wait for the other person, or will he or she wait for you, or will you continue to move ahead and still love him or her? It's really just a separation of self.

You must love yourself unconditionally.

Love doesn't hurt. We experience hurt in relationships only when we put expectations on another person and we don't get what we expect. When there are no conditions, and you realize that the pain comes from the ego and not from pure love.

With no attachment, neediness, control, manipulation, possessiveness, jealousy, or ultimatums, your heart purges until you reach a point where you do not care whether you are with the other person or not but continue to love him or her anyway.

It may look as if your twin flame is treating you badly, but it's really just your subconscious mind playing out.

Twin flames are like a reflection showing you another you.

You will notice synchronicities.

We need to heal the issues that arose from the perceived abandoning parent.

There is healing needed to be done from these deep wounds.

I had a lot to learn; I just hadn't realized it. All the human programming of the ego needed to be removed layer by layer.

During mid-March in 2018, I was just coming out of a dark night of the soul where all I wanted to do was give up. I bumped into my SP one lunchtime. Oh my God, oh shit, it was her. I hadn't seen her for years. In those few split seconds, my thoughts were "Should I go back inside? Oh my God, I've put on weight." It was too late; she'd already seen me. I said hi, and my heart was almost jumping out of my chest as she stood and chatted.

I asked the usual stuff: "Where are you living?" "Where are you working?" and such. There were a few things she said that made me think she wasn't happy. But I felt as if all my Christmases had come at once just speaking to her.

I was in for some more lessons in unconditional love.

She messaged me that evening and asked if I wanted to go for coffee sometime.

I didn't go for coffee, but I did meet her, and we talked and talked. I spoke to her every day, and about four weeks later, I was going away with Kelly and friends for the weekend. I got a message, and I could see a mirror of my own abuse replaying in her life.

My SP would turn up with her bags, get cold feet, and leave again. Again I noticed my own in-and-out energy. I was ready but not ready, if that makes any sense. I was still a gambler and wasn't ready even though I thought I was.

Our lives remained linked; she was mirroring everything I had done.

Controllers and Abusers, Manipulators and Addictions

I could see when others were controlled and emotionally manipulated. I'd even done it myself. My own gaslighting, lying to myself, and breadcrumbing of myself was also being mirrored back to me.

If you attempt to control another person's life, all it's showing you is that you have no control over your own.

We can all blame others for our actions. I have before. It was a trait I was given lessons to overcome.

Self-awareness is when we question ourselves. Most people don't question themselves. It's often easier to blame others.

We had got some tickets for us to go to a Christmas concert and another concert. It got to December, and I hadn't been to either. In hindsight, I should have walked away, but I didn't. There was an intense karmic energy.

I was upset, which is an understatement. This, on my part, was due to an utter lack of self-worth. We teach people how to treat us.

We booked a holiday, but lockdown hit, and our holiday got cancelled and was rearranged for the next year. Our holiday was eventually cancelled twice because of the continued lockdown. We bought Céline Dion tickets. The concert got rescheduled a few times, and we were supposed to see her in April 2022, but it was rescheduled again, then cancelled. Perhaps I should give up concerts.

Being controlled and abused is insidious. I didn't even know I was being abused. I went to see a medium shortly after my dad died. He said, "You're being abused, aren't you?"

But I was so unawakened at that point that I just looked at him and said, "No, I'm not." But when I got home, all of a sudden everything was so clear and made sense. The universe does indeed work in mysterious ways.

How could I not have seen it? My eyes were wide shut!

If you look at your own parents and your partner's parents, you might see a pattern.

During this time, I didn't know where I stood, and my communication skills had gone to zero. My trigger was not knowing where I stood. It was total confusion.

The more I hated myself, the worse it got; I was so unawakened then.

I'd always seen myself as a glass-half-full kind of girl, but if your life isn't going well, trust me, your beliefs are glass half empty. It carried on and on when I had this addiction that I never thought I would get rid of. In my opinion, gained from experience, the addiction will leave when we experience self-love. I was learning this.

Love does conquer all; it is the most powerful force in the universe.

We've all seen somebody in a relationship that we knew they should get out of and said, "Why don't they just leave?" Honestly, when you're in one of these relationships, it feels as if you are brainwashed. You're walking on eggshells, fearing the emotional outbursts, fearing the threats that have been made, abandoning yourself to dance to somebody else's tune.

I felt as though I had a lot of broken promises over the years from different people.

These types of relationships just show us how we feel about ourselves.

We had tickets to go to a festival in August 2022. I was looking forward to going, but again something happened and we weren't able to go. This was the straw that broke the camel's back.

It got to Christmas, and I felt as if I were hanging on by a thread. One of my Christmas presents was something that my SP had ordered for Halloween, but it didn't arrive in time. It was a photo frame of a Christmas film, and it said "love never dies." Love doesn't die, but we are given the gift of obstacles to overcome. After all, the path to true love is never easy.

Excuses

> Stubbornness is the strength of the weak.
> —Johann Kaspar Lavate

    I'd heard every excuse there possibly could be over the years—words with no actions. My communication skills were a 1 on a scale of 1 to 10. I'd get mad if I never got a straight answer to anything I'd asked. I felt as if someone had been dangling a carrot and I was the donkey. My heart hurt and was heavy with pain, and that was the trigger for my gambling. I was responsible for my own actions, but emotional abuse was my trigger.

    Stubbornness was another lesson I needed to learn about. But it was my stubbornness and my cutting my nose off to spite my face that had kept me away from my SP all those years. Also, I was not in my feminine energy but rather in my wounded energy, and I could cut things with my tongue.

    Each one learns lessons here. But I was too hurt to think about that.

    What I hadn't realized fully at that point was that the outer world just reflects one's inner world. It was obvious I was going to see chaos until I had cleared some of the negative energy from inside.

    These days I will never be too stubborn to forgive.

    I'd notice control issues in other people's lives. They were issues I could see, yet I still failed to look at myself.

    One Saturday evening, I got a call, and I knew something was the matter. There'd been an incident which was just like me so many years ago, it mirrored a similar experience, and I knew I had to heal it.

    I was on my emotional roller coaster every couple of weeks. I couldn't trust myself, and it was just being reflected. Painfully.

    The pain was intolerable, and I was using my default coping mechanisms.

Some of these were not good for my health, and some were not good for my pocket, yet I repeatedly used them. The coping mechanisms we use are for short-term relief and are like putting a plaster on a massive wound; they just don't work.

The Universe Works in Mysterious Ways

Why was I self-sabotaging so much? I had done this so many times that I decided just to ask the universe to help me. Why was I doing this to myself? The same reason any addict does it to himself or herself—to numb the pain. My gift was wrapped in sandpaper, because every time I self-sabotaged from that moment on, I didn't win anything. When I used to win while gambling, it would continue for a longer period of time. This time I would simply lose. I had already read about the twelve steps for addiction. Sometimes you just have to trust in a higher power; we have to forgive ourselves and have compassion for ourselves for using the only shitty coping mechanisms that we had found at the time.

The answer to why this was happening to me or why I was doing this was simply because, as is the case with any addiction, once I reached rock bottom, the only way was up. And up it was, and I didn't care whether it was going to be like climbing Jacob's ladder. I realized that my lack of self-love played a part in everything in my life. My own self-hatred was affecting everything: my relationships, my emotional balance (or lack thereof), my health, and my relationship with my family.

It takes courage to look at yourself in a new light, to admit that you've hurt others along the way, and to admit that you've lied and done things you shouldn't have because of addiction. You've put things at risk, and the shame you feel is one of the worst feelings. It's a perpetual landslide. One bad feeling leads to another and another until you have no other choice than to move up.

There were plenty of times when using the unhealthy coping mechanism of gambling, was so bad that I felt as if I was never going to repeat the experience and when I did it again, the guilt and shame were again unbearable.

So many times, I told myself I was never gambling again and so many times I did. I was betraying and lying to myself. I realized that if I was doing that to myself, how could I expect to be treated differently by somebody else.

Our inner thoughts and feelings create what we experience in reality. What is within, meaning inside our hearts, will show up in our reality. As above, meaning what's inside our minds, will also show up in our reality. Therefore, keeping our minds and hearts full of only what we want to experience is paramount. When you squeeze a lemon, you get lemon juice; you don't get orange juice. If someone squeezes somebody who is full of hate, that's exactly what they will get, they won't get love. Try squeezing someone full of jealousy; they won't get anything else but that. You get my drift.

Forgiveness

Forgiveness was never a trait I had in my armour. But it was one I had been given lessons for over the years, though many times I didn't realize how important it was. It felt as though no matter how many times anyone said sorry, it would never have been good enough. None of us are perfect, and we have all made shitty decisions in our lives.

These days, forgiveness is a gift.

It was spring, and I went for bottomless brunch with a group of friends. After copious amounts of prosecco and cocktails, I was speaking to the girls over the table. Jess was in a caring role, and I told her that she was an empath. She had had a relationship with a narcissist who was just as bad as the ones I had been given. I say "given" as they are just another present wrapped in sandpaper.

I spoke about forgiveness and said that to truly move on, you have to forgive.

I was more forgiving now. I had had a few lessons in this, and it's extremely cathartic. I wasn't angry about much any more. If anything, I'd looked towards finding the lessons in the experiences rather than being eaten up by them any more.

I thought I'd learned the lessons I had to learn through this, but there were still more lessons to learn—more than I realized. I lent Jess one of my books—*The Power of Now*, by Eckhart Tolle. After she read that and discussed it—obviously it was one of my favourite things to talk about (books, spirituality, life, and solving problems)—and totally got the book, she shared some different perspectives with me. She had a lot of differences in opinions to me and didn't believe in chakras at the time. She believed in more scientific stuff. I believed that what we let into our consciousness is what we see in reality, and at the time she was sceptical of this view.

The next book was "The Untethered Soul", by Michael Singer. Kelly had given me this book after she had read it; Kelly and I started reading books like this years ago.

I had closed my heart to a lot of things. That is what happens when you try to avoid pain. Paradoxically, it only causes more pain. I was learning this slowly but surely. After all, Rome surely was not built in a day.

Forgiving meant letting go of guilt and shame: the shame of my harmful coping mechanisms over the years, and the guilt of things that occurred when I was younger. Sometimes even the frustration of knowing all of the inner work I had done but still had left to do would drive me to those harmful coping mechanisms. I felt impatience about not learning it quickly enough. I was always wishing I was somewhere else, further along, more healed. I was never in the now moment, and I certainly was not trusting the process.

I experienced sad feelings, helplessness, and pain regarding not knowing how to let things go. Michael Singer's books shone a light on some of the things I had missed or forgotten. Michael Singer released a new book, and I couldn't wait to read it. He writes of meditation, surrender, chakras, and samskaras.

In Indian philosophy, samskaras are mental impressions, recollections, or psychological imprints. Samskaras run our lives unconsciously. Meditation can release them, inner-child healing, and forgiveness. After such release, you are no longer holding on to that negative energy that causes the samskaras.

Jess had previously said that she didn't believe in chakras, and to be honest, years ago I thought they were total rubbish when I first found out about them. Something told me to keep reading about them, and the more I learned about them, the more I knew I needed to work on my lower chakras.

The ideal state would be to have your chakra system, especially your heart chakra, completely open.

After reading the books, Jess was more open to chakras; and it was interesting, as my top three chakras were more open and her lower three chakras were more open and balanced. With her different perspectives, I learned that I had become good at forgiving others but not myself, and she was the opposite.

Chakra System and Meditation

> Calmness of mind is one of the
> beautiful jewels of wisdom.
> —James Allen

Many traditions have long recognized the complex chakra system and the subtle energy centres of the human body called chakras, which in Sanskrit means "wheels" or "circles".

Crown Chakra (Sahasrara)

Connection to the divine
Purple/pink
The highest chakra represents our ability to be fully connected spiritually.
Located at the very top of the head
Emotional issues: inner and outer beauty
Our connection to spirituality, pure bliss
Physical associations: pineal gland, brain, nervous system

Third Eye Chakra (Ajna)

Intuition, sense of purpose and direction in life
Purple
Our ability to focus on and see the bigger picture.
Located at the forehead between the eyes

Emotional issues: intuition, imagination, wisdom, and our ability to think and make decisions.
Physical associations: pituitary gland, eyes, and sinuses

Throat Chakra (Vishuddha)

Self-expression
Blue
Our ability to communicate
Located at the throat
Emotional issues: communication, self-expression of feelings, the truth
Physical associations: thyroid, respiratory system, teeth, and vocal cords

Heart Chakra (Aanahata)

Love, relationships, and self-acceptance.
Green
Our ability to love
Located at the centre of the chest just above the heart
Emotional issues: love, joy, and inner peace
Physical associations: heart, thymus, lower lungs, circulatory system, and immune system

Solar Plexus Chakra (Manipura)

Personal power and ability to channel
Yellow
Our ability to be confident and in control of our lives
Located in the upper abdomen in the stomach area
Emotional issues: self-worth, self-confidence, and self-esteem
Physical associations: central nervous system, pancreas, liver, digestive tract, and skin

Sacral Chakra (Swadhisthana)

Sexuality and pleasure
Orange
Our connection and ability to accept others and new experiences
Located in the lower abdomen, about two inches below the navel and two inches in
Emotional issues: sense of abundance, well-being, pleasure, and sexuality
Physical association: reproductive organs, kidneys, bowels, and immune system

Root Chakra (Muladhara)

Career, money, mindset, and sense of belonging
Red
Represents our foundation and feeling of being grounded
Located at the base of the spine in the tailbone area
issues: survival issues, such as financial independence, money, and food
Physical association: spine, rectum, legs, arms, and circulatory system

You can either continue to deny that chakras exist, or you can work with them, awaken them, clear and balance them, and have the subtle energies of them flowing freely and easily through your body. There are so many ways to clear them. You can clear them through meditation, subliminal meditation, yoga, going out in nature, reiki, sound healing, or simply talking about them and how you feel. You can also just imagine clearing them in your head. After all, it's just an energy, and that can be cleared by thought alone.

Meditation is one of the best ways to heal and balance your chakras. When you meditate and focus on the breath, you are bringing your attention to the present moment. This helps you release any stress or anxiety that is holding an energetic space in your body. The basic idea is that when your chakras are out of balance, the imbalance can lead to stress, anxiety, and depression. Meditation is being in tune with your inner universe.

The seven chakras go up along the spine to the top of the head, each of them associated with a different colour and representing a different element of your life, as you can see above. Their being out of balance can cause issues with focus, mood, and health.

Meditation can become one of your life's greatest mental health assets.

We are our own healers.

The goal isn't to control your thoughts; it's to stop the thoughts controlling you!

Letting Go

Learn to be calm and you will always be happy.
—Paramhansa Yogananda

I was in emotional pain, and I had been on the roller coaster for so long I didn't know how to get off. I had become accustomed to breadcrumbs, and that's what I got. You can't keep everybody happy all of the time.

Everything that happened was like a mirror of years ago. And it was in my face, so I knew I had to heal it.

I had gone back for the kids, but it was a big mistake.

Things happened that I'd have liked clarity on, but I got told to believe what I wanted to believe.

Oh, I obviously didn't like the answer, and I tried hard not to let my mind torture me, but it did, because that's what the mind does, and I had to find a way to make it stop. Remembering the power of now, I had to try to be present all times. This was hard, and doing so takes practice, but I look forward to the day I am a whole lot more peaceful. That is exactly what a spiritual practice is; it takes practice.

I had to adopt radical acceptance of what was.

I felt a sense of powerlessness and meaninglessness during the months to follow, and powerlessness anchors itself into the psyche. I felt I'd gone on a downward spiral as I headed into another dark night of the soul.

My mind was running away with itself, and it was torturous.

My mind continued to make my life what could be described only as a living hell.

We all end up having a negative trait of a caregiver, I think. I woke up ready to go to work, and I was like a cat on a hot tin roof. I'm guessing that if I were bipolar, I would have been going through a manic stage. Nothing made sense to me. It was the morning my SP met me to say goodbye. I found myself saying the same words she did years prior.

I went to work that morning, and I don't know how I was even there, because I didn't really feel like I was. I was calm, but I was dying inside. The months after that were excruciatingly painful and unbelievably unbearable, and if I'd never walked through the sweet valley of hell before, I surely was now. The separation was like burning in a fire—so extremely painful. It mirrored the same separation we had experienced years before, but opposite.

I had to figure out why my relationships were like this. I had to go over everything I'd read before, obviously I had attachment issues. according to Tolle, when we are attached to something, it causes us pain.

When we have deep unhealed core wounds, we relive them time and time again until we heal them.

Things were starting to make sense, and over the coming months I discovered the issues were not only my lack of self-love but also my core wounds, and I set about to get to the bottom of these.

Every single relationship I'd ever had started off okay and ended with a devaluation stage, and I came to understand that the reason this happens is through lack of self-love. Basically, the other person is saying to you, "If you don't love yourself and respect yourself, then why the hell should I?"

Over the years, I've seen so many people destroy themselves through drink, drugs, and other addictions through their lack of self-love. I could see this clearly now.

I looked at my undesirable behaviours over the years and began to heal them too.

Narcissists act like the biggest victims in the world. They will insidiously take control of your life with overt commands, demands, and threats. It's dangerous, because they will slowly but surely eradicate your identity.

I'd been with someone exactly like that, and I was brainwashed to the point that my life didn't feel like my own.

I had found over the years that the information I needed at any particular time would come along, be it in the shape of a book, YouTube video, or conversation with somebody.

On my YouTube feed, I found Madea's life-changing speech called "Let Them Go". If people want to walk out of your life, let them go.

The video is well worth a listen to.

I had certainly lacked boundaries over the years, and I also had regrets about things I'd done in the past that were stopping me from even beginning to love myself.

We have to forgive ourselves and accept the experiences that shaped us before we can even begin to love ourselves.

There came a time when I had been shown so many times what I was lacking that there was only one thing I could really do, and that was love myself. It was not some overnight process, unbeknown to me.

It wasn't like years ago, when I used rebound tactics to fill in the gaping hole left in my heart, only to build a deeper, darker hole in my soul, leaving damage that only connecting to my soul could heal.

The only way out was through, and I had to crawl through the valley of pain to hopefully rise like a Phoenix from the ashes.

I no longer wanted relationships in which the other person told me he or she loved me but treated me as though he or she hated me. I no longer wanted to be gaslighted, love-bombed, used, abused, treated poorly, breadcrumbed, or ghosted.

But all this started with me. That was exactly how I was treating myself. Self-love had to become the most important goal now.

As a feminine person who'd gone round and round in circles, not knowing my own worth and letting myself be treated appallingly, it was time to get out of my own ditch—my own self-made gutter.

You have to become the four-legged version of yourself. One that isn't going to topple and turn to shitty coping mechanisms to numb the pain. Strength is key, and I was going to find it—inner strength—through meditation, self-soothing, inner peace, and self-love.

I was not going to be my own worst enemy.

I had been a menace to my own destiny.

Oftentimes our own worst enemy is our own minds.

Through conversations with my friends, they reminded me how I forgive others but not myself. I saw different perspectives, and I recognized that I never forgave myself for anything and carried massive regret (which, by the way, is seriously heavy).

I was talking about transcendental meditation, and Jess said she'd like to try it. She found a lady who teaches it where we lived, which was unusual; not many have a teacher like that on their doorstep. I took it as a sign and decided to do it.

It took me a long while to totally get to grips with "True happiness lies within."

I wasn't new to meditation but had struggled to quiet my mind over the years, I'd practised and practised. Then I'd given up, thinking it wasn't working, though it actually was, and became disheartened. I went through this cycle multiple times. The soul speaks when the mind is quiet.

Not doing the inner work is like not watering a plant. In the latter case, the plant dies. So no wonder it often felt like two steps forward and one back. Hence the frustration and the vicious cycle of not being where I wanted to be.

It didn't feel like one truth to me then; it felt like a great big jigsaw puzzle.

I had a knowing that I'd nearly finished that puzzle.

Over the years I have learnt about forgiveness. I had found ho'oponopono, the simple ancient Hawaiian forgiveness prayer. It's very powerful, and if you've never heard of it, maybe try and read about it.

It goes as follows:

> I'm sorry
> Please forgive me
> Thank you
> I love you

It's about taking responsibility for everything that affects your state of being. It's the art of acceptance, forgiveness, and cleansing the energies that you attract into your life.

There were a few times I said I wished I wasn't here. I changed my perspective, and I'd read Michael Singer's book in which he explains how lucky we really are to be here. His book *The Untethered Soul* was a learning experience in itself.

I love how he makes others see what the hidden problem really is—how we build apparatuses around us to protect ourselves. It's a paradox.

Narcissistic and Codependent Behaviour

A short and sweet chapter as we do not want to muddy our minds with these behaviours. I will use "narcissist" and "codependent" not as labels but to name the behaviours, as there are different levels of each.

Obviously, I have studied a lot of these kinds of behaviours.

As I've said previously, it's like a dance of wounded souls. *Codependence: The Dance of Wounded Souls* was one of the first books I read by Robert Burney as I was searching for information on my own codependency when I found myself lost.

The one needs the other. The codependent must learn to stand on his or her own two feet, to have boundaries and nonattachment, and to heal wounds from the past. The narcissist finds the codependent to enable him or her to see the codependent behaviour. They find each other energetically, as that is what attracts them to each other. The codependent, in his or her victim mentality, must not be the victim, the fixer, or the enabler. He or she must rise up to be the best possible version of himself or herself.

We can be codependent with narcissistic traits or very narcissistic with codependent traits. It's wounded masculine and feminine energy playing out.

I came to understand these dynamics and looked at how my whole family played out the dysfunctional dance. It was very enlightening.

Some presents are wrapped in sandpaper, as Lisa Nichols says.

I'd often thought there must be a reason why this happens.

There are no therapeutic cures for narcissism, unfortunately, as the dynamic needs the codependent to learn from until the energies are balanced. It can be healed only through strength and love, not by trying to fix or enabling. If you show weakness, you've lost your power. The relationship forces you to look inside of yourself, to love yourself, to find strength, and to set boundaries.

Narcissism is unrequited self-love. The empath or codependent has also closed her heart, but the dynamic is different. Both suffer shame, lack of self-love, poor boundaries, control-seeking, fear of intimacy, and denial. The empath usually sees the good in others but never herself.

They are like two halves of the same coin. The narcissist usually has the worse reputation, but the codependent is not always innocent within the dynamic. The mother and father wound plays a role in this too. If there is no wound, then the dynamic cannot play out.

Then there is the insidious covert abuse, which I have insight into, yet I have a more positive outlook on it than in years past. Hidden emotional abuse is hard to detect even by oneself. We can't see it, because it's familiar, and we can sit comfortably in it. We get gaslit so much over the years that we doubt our own reality. But eventually, after we are sucked dry of any life force we have and are feeling like empty shells, we rise. We do the cycle again, either with the same person or someone else, if the lesson isn't learnt. We've walked on eggshells and fended off angry outbursts and certainly never rocked the boat. Our nerves are raw, and our souls feel destroyed as we wonder how it can happen to us.

We can choose self-love. We can learn boundaries and assertiveness. We just haven't got those tools in our armour yet.

We learn to say no. We refuse to sacrifice ourselves for others. We do what's best for *us!*

Shame and Vulnerability

My go-to for this was the marvellous Brené Brown.

We struggle to be vulnerable. This can be quite tough, as you may know if you've never been vulnerable. Sometimes it's easier and more comfortable to be clever or joke or ignore than to be vulnerable.

That feeling of fear inside us makes us feel as if we aren't good enough and as if we are unworthy. For me, it led to unhealthy coping mechanisms, unhealthy relationships, and addiction.

I'd worked through the twelve steps. I won't go into all of them, as you can find them if you wish. But step one says, "We admitted that we are powerless and that our lives had become unmanageable." Step two says, "Come to believe that a power greater than us could restore us to a normal way of thinking and living." Admit it to yourself and be ready to have the defects of character removed and to remove your shortcomings. The last step says, "Carry the message to others."

The more I let go and let God and trusted in a higher power, the more addiction left my life.

I found that willpower will not work. We are essentially powerless.

What I found was that no one ever asked me about my gambling. Fear drove others not to ask. I knew this because I never asked the addicts in my own life about their addictions. They thought that if they buried their heads, it would go away. I did that too.

I'd looked for the lesson in gambling, as there is a lesson in everything. But without risk, you can never win.

Very true indeed. These days, any risk I take will be in my life.

We cannot continue to protect our hearts out of fear of getting hurt. We cannot continue to wear the uncomfortable apparatus that Michael

Singer describes in his book The Untethered Soul. Life just becomes more uncomfortable.

It is often said that the universe never gives us more than we can handle, even though at times that hasn't felt like the case. It is true. There have been times when I thought the pain was far too great to handle. This required me to have total faith and trust in the universe.

The universe always has a plan.

Yes, it took me years to understand this.

Faith and Manifestation

> The mind is in its own place, and in itself can
> make a heaven of hell, a hell of heaven.
> —John Milton

Neville Goddard became one of my favourite authors in faith and manifestation.

I didn't understand the saying "As above, so below" or "As within, so without."

Our imagination is our greatest power. Obviously, I'd used mine to create unwanted scenarios over and over.

We can use our energy for worry or belief; it's up to us which wolf we feed. Imagination is everything; it manifests.

Buddha said, "What you think you become. What you feel you attract. What you imagine you create."

I was first introduced to the law of attraction years ago when I was doing a course and the assessor apologized for being late and stated that her daughter had had a flat tyre. She said this was due to the law of attraction, as she always talked about getting a flat tyre. She told me about the book by Rhonda Byrne. I got it from the library and read it, and I then knew there was more to life. I went on to buy a whole selection of law of attraction books.

I watched everything with Wayne Dyer in it and bought a number of his books. There is more to the universe than meets the eye.

Our subconscious minds are extremely powerful. They have tremendous power in controlling our life experiences, including our levels of income, the actions we take every day, and how we react to stress.

We have to be aware of what we are planting into our subconscious minds. They have stored information from the past and continue to store it today. They're where our beliefs are stored. The "I'm unworthy" belief can be reprogrammed. We all have limiting beliefs that can be reprogrammed.

There are twelve laws of the universe, including eleven hidden laws that you can use to improve your life.

We are cocreators of our own reality.

Develop self-love and self-worth as soon as you can. When I realized that I'd manifested through my own beliefs, thoughts, and energy nothing but breadcrumbing, gaslighting, being unheard, betrayal, and abandonment, I had already done all of those things to myself in my mind. It wasn't my fault, but it was now my responsibility to clean this mess up. Bitterness and jealousy are all a lack of self-love.

> "The truth will set you free."
> John 8:32

Anthony Hopkins speaks beautiful words of wisdom in a poem entitled "Let Go of the People Who Aren't Ready to Love You Yet." You can read it here: Beautiful Words of Wisdom from Anthony Hopkins (drhurd.com)

Healing

I had done a lot of meditation and healing and learning about self-awareness and trying to be more self-aware, but I was still using unhealthy coping mechanisms, and I'd still react rather than respond. But what I learnt was that I had come quite far even though it seemed I wasn't getting anywhere. I'd been impatient but now realized it was a process. And it wasn't going to happen overnight. It's lifelong. I hadn't given myself credit. I was much better at controlling my strong emotions even if I did still have an active addiction. They used to come flying out like wood coming out of a wood chipper. I had learned through meditation to calm my mind more. I'd learnt a lot, but I was laying the foundation.

People learn how to treat us by what we do or do not accept. Even if that person loves you and you think you don't need them, you do.

The secret is to find your unhealed wounds and heal them. This was easier said than done.

The more you resist the lessons in life, the more you'll get.

Yes, I was a resistor!

I thought I could just carry on with my coping mechanisms instead of putting in the work. It didn't work. I knew I had to try and stay present in the present moment more. Doing this is hard to get your head around at first, and it takes practice, but what doesn't?

I never wanted to get on that roller coaster again.

I had to heal issues with my body. God forbid anyone saw it. I had issues with self-love, unworthiness, addiction, and attachment issues. We all have a mother and father wound to find and heal. Looking at this, it seems a lot to heal. Healing doesn't cause self-actualization, but self-actualization causes healing. I'd taken the long road of trying to fix everything first. It seemed impossible and exhausting.

I think the universe had enough of me messing about, and I heard something regarding my SP that I really didn't want to hear and that was the catalyst to my biggest awakening yet. If I thought my heart hurt before, this was one thousand times worse, and it pushed me to get out of the pain. Honestly, I was numb. Then I wished I was numb because the pain was unbearable, and I cannot tell you how unbearable it was.

I'll add some notes from my journal from this period. I achieved more in that space of time during my meditations than I had for eighteen years. It was the hardest, most brutal thing I have ever been through. Little did I know that I was going to see the truth and that the truth was that everything I saw in my reality, I was. It was like seeing myself through others' eyes. I could see all my wrongdoings and my shadow side, and it's hard to look at your anger, your jealousy, your fears, your limiting beliefs, your codependency, and your lack of self-worth, but you also see your good stuff, the stuff you ignored when focusing on the negative.

My Journal

Week 1

The insurmountable pain I was feeling was off the scale. I was incapacitated, similar to when my dad died, and numb from head to toe. And for a while I wondered if I'd be able to live the rest of my days with this severe emotional pain. I needed to be whole and be in soul and stay out of my mind and ego. That became the main focus as I tried so hard not to let my mind run away with thoughts of "Everything's fucked", and I just couldn't let them in … not only because the pain was so bad if I did but also because I knew I had to stay in soul and become the strongest I had ever been, and if I wasn't broken before, this was trying to break me. But I thought, "Fuck you. I've come this far, and you will not be breaking me now." I had to stay in the now every single moment until it had become the norm, and I knew that even before, when I was being pushed, the mind and ego still were free to roam, and this was evidently the push that was going to make sure I stayed in soul. And it was the biggest challenge of my life, and I heard the only way out is through, and I knew it. I was pleased I was off work as I navigated what felt like the largest obstacle of my life, but I refused to sit in pain or focus on anything other than myself … I mattered. I was focusing heavily on my own well-being and self-worth and self-love. Hard to love yourself? My recommendation is to start before you get a really great big kick right up the backside. There're two roads, but really you come to a point where there's no choice, as you will not go down that dark road again … so you head towards the light and shed and let go of anything that no longer serves you—the anger, the inferno inside, the envy, the lack of self-worth—and then you come to a place where you know you are worthy and lovable and wanted, and the universe will mirror this. This latest thing had just shown me I was massively out of alignment with love. Unconditional love. I had been brainwashed and protected my abusers, and it was clear it was a mirror. I had felt trapped yet could have walked away, but due to my feelings of lack and unworthiness, it made it nearly impossible to leave until it repeated over and over again until I saw it clearly. I had to forgive myself for my naivety and immaturity and let go of my attachments and abandonment wounds once and for all. And this meant being in soul *all* of the time, regardless of what was showing up—no preferences, judgements, or expectations—and it was tough for the ego to get this. But I was entering the new earth come hell or high water. Yes, it was easier said than done! You have to learn to be present every single moment.

Tonight I heard in meditation that we have to anchor in new energies.

I had an awful feeling as I thought about my lessons and the pain of the feeling of loss. The feeling of helplessness. And you just want that pain in the pit of your stomach to disappear. I then thought I should have learned my lesson sooner, again beating myself up for not being perfect or rising to the challenge before now. This is the mind and ego versus the soul. It becomes a vicious cycle as you relive the pain over and over, all the while trying to stay present. I knew I needed to heal from the inside out for the pain to stop. At this point, I oscillated from feeling better to worse over and over again. I knew I had to balance this energy.

I knew I had gone through various awakenings over the years, and as tough as those ones were, they were of a far gentler disposition than the one I seemed to be going through now. It had brought me to my knees, blindfolded and wrists bound. It was an inner strength that I needed now, but this time with everything I had in me.

We choose to come here to earth to overcome challenges for the purpose of our souls' expansion. We are always doing this regardless of whether we know we are or not. Our egos and personalities will be tested until we find inner strength. It's a test for us to love ourselves to our core. We have to have boundaries, love ourselves very deeply, and trust in the universe. As we fight with our inner demons over and over, we develop a resilience we never had before. I decided that nothing was ever going to interrupt my peace again, and I meant it. I was going to become unshakable.

Seriously though, when we neutralize and balance the energy of wanting, desiring, or needing another person, we become whole. Pure consciousness. And that is where we are free. You have to mute the noise of the mind, the trauma, and the pain.

It's a process and comes through the hard lessons we get to learn and the letting go of anger, jealousy, resentment, and our attachments of anything. I saw a video the other day of a fly trap holding tight to something, and that's attachment right there. No wonder whoever you have attached yourself to wants to escape. It's pretty uncomfortable.

It's not easy facing all of those things and letting them go. The whole process can last lifetimes.

I was shown my masculine wound in detail. I hadn't realized how big it was. It was huge. I'd only been focusing on my mother wound. I couldn't really believe it; I'd only seen what I wanted to see. My mind had constructed a story—a great, big, fat horrible story that just went on to repeat itself over and over with both wounds mirrored to me by others. The original wounds of perceived abandonment, betrayal, physical abuse, rejection, and emotional unavailability were topped off with all of them being re-enacted in each subsequent relationship, piling more of the shit on the original wound, making it harder to clear, and I chose not to see it. Then it made total sense why I had developed my addiction; that was made clear to see too. I developed my gambling addiction in my early thirties. I say "developed", but it actually peaked; I already had it. I knew then why things had happened the way that they had. All of my relationships have been karmic. When I lost my dad, I had a very powerful karmic who showed me pretty much every wound I had. But being strong isn't always best. The sting from that wasn't enough to make me surrender. However, it was strong enough to make me reach for my addictions even more. Obviously for me, the heavier the pain, the crazier the addiction. But who better than yourself in a twin flame mirror to know what is going to drive you deep into the pits of despair. We chose to do it before we came here, and I knew I had, and I just had to surrender. I heard there's nothing here for you to cling onto, it's all transient, and for all I'd heard it before, I didn't get it, and now I knew it to be true. We are all so much bigger than this.

I hadn't looked at myself fully, but here I was, more shadows coming up like tidal waves, and I'd close my eyes tight so I couldn't see them, because I knew I would have the work of healing to do. I subconsciously knew, and I knew it would be tough, so I resisted. I was reminded of my T-shirt all those years ago that said "I am a menace to my own destiny." We all are. We do anything to not feel the pain.

I was then shown why I had had my previous dark nights of the soul, and that was so this dark night of the soul wasn't too big—and it was enormous. But it could have been worse had I not had the previous ones. My nervous system was shot to pieces, and I realized how my parents felt. I could feel it. Perhaps they never really got to look inside deeply to get rid of the wound. Fortunately, I'd already lessened some of the karma I had by releasing samskaras over the years in meditation, and I'd worked on forgiveness and let at least a tiny bit go, but I still knew that this was the core wounds that were going to come out. There was no other way unless I wanted to die, basically. The only way out is through.

There was a pain in my heart chakra, and I could hardly bear it. I just needed peace, total inner peace.

The pain was worse than I felt when my dad had died. I didn't think it was possible, but this time I knew I was being forced into my soul and had to have total trust in the universe. I felt sick to my stomach, I had extreme pain and my ego / mind was fighting me like hell. I was going to try to stay connected to source / be in soul / one with the universe / in the present moment for as long as I could, but it was like I was fighting all of my demons all at once, and the heavy feeling of anxiety, depression, withdrawal symptoms, and deep grief all at the same time, multiplied by a hundred, and I felt like I was tearing my hair out. Obviously, I wanted to gamble, smoke, get drunk, or absolutely anything other than feel like this, but I surrendered. I couldn't take it any more. It felt like I needed an exorcist as the grief, anger, denial, and bargaining—a fireball of anxiety—all pushed up to the surface to be felt and healed. I had flashes of seeing how I had treated people unfairly and vice versa, and it was just like I could see all of my karma on a screen in front of me.

It's too painful to be in my mind/ego, so I meditated the whole day. I'd heard Wayne Dyer say when he asked Deepak Chopra how to solve a problem he'd say, "Meditate meditate meditate." So meditation it was. I'm really going all in now, even though I thought I already had. This was the universe kicking my ego up the arse with a winkle-picker, and it fucking hurt like hell. I'm going to listen to the power of now again. I MUST get out of my mind. I have to make the suffering end. I felt so hurt. I just felt all those low-level feelings, and that is not what I'm here for. I had worked on a lot of stuff years ago, only for it to all happen again, but I'd only scratched the surface. You have to go deep. Pick it out at the core. Even gambling wouldn't have taken the pain away. Not that I was willing to find out, which was a good thing. Now I knew there is only ONE way out of the pain, and I was going to do it. No matter what.

Week 2

I feel like my body was in some kind of thumbscrew, pushing and pulling, and it was painful like I had a thorn in my side. I feel like I'm under immense pressure, but I'm coming out like a shiny diamond. I'm more determined than ever to come out like that diamond. I'd listened to Anna Brown's meditation; I was doing anything I could to stay out of pain and confusion or my mind running away with itself, making me feel worse. On the one hand, I didn't think I could feel any worse, but on the other, the big, shiny diamond was going to emerge. It was like being in limbo. I HAD to feel better and finally felt like I may be getting somewhere, as I knew there'd be a tipping point. Suffering pushes you into soul. It's like there is no other choice. It was like do or die. I could have chosen alcohol or gambling or reacting with anger or any low-level coping mechanism, all of which I had chosen before, and they had just made things worse. So here I was, with a choice that was actually only one choice—and that was to become whole again. To love myself unconditionally. Anything less would be an insult to where I came from. To become the cocreator of my own reality. To never be in victim mode and rise. I heard you cannot solve a problem with the same consciousness that created it. I'd read about the four levels of consciousness, and I was going up, not down. The only way is up. There will be no more downhill spirals. I'd chosen to look at the actions people use out of pain and fear, and I noticed how I had too. I hadn't taken a good look at my pain much before now; I'd just buried it. And now it was spewing out like sewerage all over, and I had to clean it up. Everything in my reality had been cocreated by me, my thoughts, my feelings, my beliefs, my vibration, and my actions. I knew this, but the more I was shown, the harder it was hard to stomach. It may have looked like I was a victim sometimes from the outside, but no, it was all me. I'd created it, and the souls in my life were just mirroring back to me my inner state. It was time to clear this shit up and create anew. I'd got to this point, and I had plenty of souls not just showing me the bad stuff but showing me the good too. I had people in my life with good hearts and love, kindness, and support, yet over the years I only focused on the bad, and that just created more. It felt uncomfortable, like I was out of my comfort zone. I realized that's why we push people away if they're too nice. It's uncomfortable.

I saw stress, anxiety, depression, and pain daily, and I thought, "This cannot be all there is here." Everyone was stressed and miserable. People were having meltdowns, breakdowns, and in a lot of pain. Even as a child I thought that there had to be more to life. I was right; it just took a little while to realize. Like forty plus years, for fuck's sake. I looked from a different perspective, from soul. Time doesn't exist, and I remembered the butterfly my SP drew with the words "time flies" in the middle, where its body was. In that moment, I felt at one with the universe, with everything, like a samadhi moment. This is unity consciousness, and to stay there you have to practise and keep feeling your way into it. It can't be explained, just experienced. A couple of days ago, I heard Jim Carrey say pretty much the same thing—how he had experienced this and wished he could get there again. I knew exactly what he meant. There'll come a time when you can enter that state in a millisecond. Now I understood the practice I'd been doing. It was simple but not easy. If I could just get to that millisecond mark. But we ARE that; it just needs uncovering. It's just under the surface of the conditioning and programming. Being one with the universe. Being one and not feeling the pain body, not feeling anxiety, jealousy, hatred, anger, and attachment, and free from codependency and attacks from narcissistic individuals. Only love and peace survive in that space. I had seen a post earlier that said, "The journey of a thousand miles starts with one step." Obviously, I wanted to be on my thousandth mile, but it's a pathless path and you never know what's coming next. Our minds keep saying, "When will it end? Are we there yet?" But the only way to deal with that is through presence. This is where you are free. Staying there and balancing that energy isn't easy. The freedom is the feeling we wanted all along. It's not material things we need; it's the feeling of peace. And everything else will follow.

I'd never really felt peace. Even as a child, I bit my fingers to the bone and could never sit still for a moment.

I sat thinking how we get swept away by someone's words that aren't followed by actions. We've all been there. It's about watching the actions, not listening to the words. Yet words can be so alluring. Actions prove who someone is, while words are just who they pretend to be.

Anyway, I was listening to a podcast. The masculine energy mirrors the feminine. It mirrors her self-worth or lack of it. So as the alcoholic or addict abandons themselves, this will be mirrored by the masculine by them abandoning her. She's down a well with no visible way out, and she can either slip down even further or crawl her way up, no matter how, with courage and determination. I could see the ones who've slipped further down, and God knows I'd slipped down there many times. We aren't here for fun, just lessons and our souls' expansion. At work I liked a lot of people, but there were people who tested me relentlessly. Working with the public has diminished my compassion somewhat. I'd seen them fighting and arguing in queues, lying, stealing, and lacking patience and gratitude. There was nothing nice about it, but on the other side of the coin—which there will always be—it's opposite. We had so many gifts and cards of appreciation, yet the things we really remember are the not-so-good ones. I will never focus on the not so good.

I'd been building my emotional strength muscle over the years; nothing had come close to the pain I was feeling here. It was loss—loss of control and the feeling of unworthiness, uncertainty, and just everything coming to the surface—and I knew it was a test. I hated this test, but that's duality, and I had to practise radical acceptance, which was hard, but I was determined to do it. I had to be zen, be soul, be present, or my ego mind would just torture me, and I may as well be dead and buried. Alcohol was not enough to escape the emotional pain, and I decided I was not drinking in the house again. When we're in pain, we all wonder, "Why is this happening to me?" There are four levels of consciousness, and simply by asking, "Why is this happening to me," you are in victim consciousness. I knew this, and I wanted to be at the top level of consciousness, where I was unaffected by anything or anyone around me. I'm not going to lie;

it was tough, as the mind kept saying things like "It's your fault" and "If only you'd done this, that, or the other." We all know this scenario, and we've all listened to that voice in our head. But I was awakening and had become the observer of my mind, and I saw the thoughts come and go, and I was learning to let them go rather than allowing my mind to make up more stories. I was wise enough now to know the damage it could do, and it had done enough. My lack of self-love had been reflected back to me so much, and it was hard to bear. So self-love and self-acceptance it was going to have to be. I never, ever wanted to feel like crap to that extent again. I had to get my mind, body, and soul into alignment, treating them all with the respect they deserved. The fight was on. I said, "Bring it on," and bring it on the universe did. Little did I know the pain that was to follow, but here we were. The phrase "brought me to my knees" was literal. That pain had me begging and pleading with God / the universe / the divine / higher power to just please alleviate this emotional pain.

Now I really knew what being a menace to my own destiny meant; however, I was feeling like I was in a transitory period and becoming whole. It was annoying, and I can't really explain it, but my heart felt a little freer and there was no pain, and I knew that love was moving inside my heart. There were energies going on all through my body at this time. I had felt them before, not often, but now I knew it was the old dense energy leaving my body. The sneaky ego mind still tried to get in, but I was seeing signs and synchronicities everywhere, and there were other reminders, too, and it seemed very extreme. I refuse to let my mind run wild, and I was definitely feeling more in my soul at this point. It felt like slow motion, like half in half out—a gradual movement. I was shown a vision of myself on a higher timeline, and that was when that saying "The only time is now" made sense.

After the initial feeling of my world collapsing in on itself, there I was, facing my fear. Face everything and rise rather than fear everything and run. The fear playing out—that I wasn't chosen, that I wasn't good enough, that I was unworthy—was an unwanted fear. It was abundantly clear that this needed to be cleared immediately. I could not stay in that vibration, and the reality was coming at me painfully. I knew I had to release all this negative energy, and that is exactly what I was going to do. My head was all over the place. I couldn't get out of the addictive energy of anything, and my soul was just not at peace. In previous years, boredom had got me doing things that I didn't really want to do, and I had to find peace. This immense pain was literally pushing me to find peace. The ego mind felt pain, and it felt damaged, but I knew this was not the reality or the truth of who I really AM.

Now the universe really wanted to play. I'd seen some text messages in my mind's eye pop up which were comforting. I was feeling a little better, like I'd shifted into a higher vibration, and I could feel it; I was more present. I now realize that if I had loved myself to my core, I could have saved myself from the pain and the agony. I could tell my twenty-year-old self a lot of truth by now. I thought, "If only I had known," but then I never would have had those experiences and wouldn't be writing about them now. By really loving yourself, you have to go deep within, connecting to the universe in silence, and it takes practice to stay in that vibration mainly because of the nonstop talking ego mind. Feeling your way into the vibration of the universe—I knew it conceptually, and I'd felt it briefly, but that is where you will find the truth and see the ego for what it really is, which is fear. Love and fear cannot coexist. There is only love. You become love. You feel it from your heart like burning embers, and it's the feeling of home. Where you've searched all your life, you are finally home, you are finally free. You know how and why everything happened the way it did as it's revealed to you. Yes, you feel battered and bruised, but you know how to be free. It's such an amazing feeling. I realized that all the feelings I had felt were exactly the same feelings that I had given myself—how I'd breadcrumbed myself, how I'd felt unworthy and unwanted, how I'd given up, how I'd betrayed myself, the lack of self-worth, the regret, the jealousy—and I knew I was almost finished with the major lessons, as the years had been constant lessons. My actual spiritual awakening had started in 2006 after I lost my dad, but I hadn't realized that that was what was happening. I can clearly see those lessons now. The months in the library reading book after book, the third parties, the addictions, the abandonment, clearly seeing how I lacked love for myself. I was the one person I was going to be with for the rest of my life, yet I treated myself so appallingly. The codependency, the addictions, the betrayals and being made to feel not good enough as I hadn't conformed—the duality was collapsing as I felt an overwhelming love for the things my mind had perceived as bad and took the lessons from them with gratitude because had it not been for those, I wouldn't be ascending. I had said to the universe, "Bring it on," and it did exactly as I asked, and I was thrust into an awakening like a tsunami. There was still work to do, as I could still feel it in my body, but I was going from feeling excited about what may come next to fearing what could or couldn't be. I couldn't rest, and I started to doubt everything. I got to see how I made people feel with my judgmental attitude, devaluing life choices, and decisions, and everything that disgusted me was something I myself had done. Then comes the anger, the regret, the thoughts of "How could I have been so stupid?" It was uncomfortable, to say the least. Everything came to the surface as I saw my reactions, my jealousy, and my spiteful game-playing. Everything I disliked about myself, which was my shadow self, was shown clearly to me and coming up like a volcano to be healed. There was no stopping it. It was tough to face, but no tougher than the last twenty years. I'd told my SP it was like she was getting back at me for the past, but I knew it was just a reflection of what needed healing inside me. I'd already recognized this and had guilt and shame, but instead of facing it and healing it, I denied it and buried it. Love heals them. Healing doesn't cause self-actualization, but self-actualization causes the healing. The long or short route. All the years looking at healing modalities, trying to release trauma and guilt tirelessly, which are all good but like diving into an abyss—you just get lost. You may feel lighter for a short period, but it was a thankless exercise for me. When you manage to get to the truth of who you are, which is love, then you heal from within. You're free and clear and have no heavy burdens weighing you down. No anxiety—which is fear—no heartache, no attachment, just love where fear can't exist. The only person who can hurt you is you. I was told this around 2007 in the spiritualist open circle. The man pointed at me and told me, and at the time I wanted to walk out, thinking, "What sort of message is that?" But it was always in the forefront of my mind. Love thy enemy, as the enemy is essentially you, your own thoughts. That's the only enemy. I had been my own worst enemy. It was intense, and I could feel that heavy energy move, and I released it back to the universe to clear and transmute across all time, dimension, space, and reality. I'd done energy clearing before, but because I didn't believe in it, it didn't work. But I knew it was real; I knew I was a multidimensional being now and only wanted to vibrate at the level of love—which on the Hawkins vibrational scale is 500. That map of consciousness was there for my goal; I didn't care about anything else but reaching 500 for now. I had developed a trust in the universe like never before. But even that was swinging on the pendulum. That map of consciousness was something for me to look at as I recalled being right down the bottom with my shame, blame, and regret. It didn't make me laugh, but I did kind of chuckle at how I could see how everything had happened to make me move up the scale.

Things were coming up every day for me to move through and heal, and it was a process that was heavy on my heart. I realized that one of my core wounds was me asking, "What if there's not enough love for me?" and I heard my mother tell me, "You used to say you love him more than me," meaning my brother. Then, when Jan came into our reality, I wondered that too, yet that lovely lady was brought up not knowing her dad, and when we met her, I knew how painful that must have been. Love is infinite. I must have been scared as a child that it was going to disappear, and in every relationship I had, it had done just that due to my fear. The shame of feeling that as a child was bad enough, but bringing it into adulthood was just insane.

I realized how spiky and prickly I was, how I used to like children but seeing them grow up caused me pain. And at some point, I decided I didn't like them much or couldn't tolerate them. I was terrified my own kids would have their own children and they'd be born into a world full of pain. I hadn't looked at it in this light from this perspective before, and neither would I have done if it hadn't have been thrust upon me. I could feel it in my lower chakras, like the anxiety and fear that had been there for so long, and I remembered someone telling me I had no rapport with kids. I didn't understand that at the time. It was another samskara to release, another thorn in my side. I wanted to go down a big hole and hide when I met children for the sheer fear of them disliking me, yet it was a limiting belief. I wasn't sure where this fear had come from, but I knew it would come to me. Then, after sitting with this, a memory came up. It seemed insignificant, but it was huge. It had created this fear in me that I was unaware of. "Terrified" was the word, and "lack of control". A baggage is held on to without knowing. Well, goodbye extra baggage.

With all these things coming up, I felt I'd been flogged five thousand times and was barely alive—a little extreme, I know, but this is what the mind does. Every day, without fail, I meditated. I could get to feeling as one with the universe, and I just wanted to stay there. It was like a balancing act.

I'd seen my chakras, and I remembered trying to spin them in the beginning when I first discovered them. But they were woo-woo then, so I gave up. But over the years, I had kept on looking at them; it was like they were gemstones embedded in a cave wall and the only way to get them out and working was to dig them out, but I only had one tool, and it was a rusty old spoon. I had become grateful for that spoon, as it was better than no tool at all. Slowly but surely, they'd be revealed and spin and align again. That was the long path, trying to get them open. The short path was surrendering and meditating; then they just opened naturally as they were revealed. My journey had been a mix of both trying to open them and them opening naturally. I had to be aware of them to know they needed healing. But all that matters is that you move forward no matter what. All paths lead home.

It was now mid-February, and I was doing okay. I was learning that when I went back to things from the past, they had started to make sense. It was a relief after all the confusion. I had to stay out of the ego mind and keep my emotions in check, and I was doing it. I was expecting a fight, a battle, and that's what I got. I'd watched *Godzilla vs. Kong*; it was kind of like that. He kept fighting Godzilla, who backed off in the end peacefully after a long, exhausting, and arduous tug of war.

I was still fighting the ego mind. It's extremely strong; it's what controls our addictions and behaviour. But again I thought, "Fuck you a thousand times." I'd just finished watching a Netflix programme about a woman drug lord, which was an enormous lesson in ego. We reap what we sow.

I'd meditated most of the day, for the simple reason that I was determined to get to where I wanted to be, which was free, and that takes practice. It's ego driven, which is the paradox, telling me to buckle up because there's somewhere to go, which causes anxiety in itself because we aren't there yet. It was like my regular chronic anxiety but turned up a good few notches, which is kind of unbearable, but it pushes you to where you need to be, because without suffering you are not inclined to move forward. The mind is constantly chattering, making you doubt your every move, saying, "You're not getting very far", "You'll never be happy", "You've got too much shit going on", "You'll never get rid of that shame." I recalled how I sold my car to pay my mortgage after gambling too much over and over. The shame is something you try to hide like a horrible skeleton in the wardrobe, but I was open about my gambling, shining a light on it so it wasn't a dark secret, and it lost its allure. Anything that has the light shone on it can't stay in the darkness. The shame was hiding in plain sight but still weighing me down, but by now I knew that an addiction was just an outer manifestation of my inner state. Chaos. The shame, the anger, the resentment for having it, the fear, the feeling of unworthiness because of it … and I thought, "For fuck's sake, I thought I'd dealt with this and released it," but no, no I hadn't. There was still a way to go, and I had a choice of the long road or the short road. The short road is connecting directly to source. All the healing modalities we all do work at a percentage not worth bothering with; it's hard work, and time consuming. Don't try to do things with the ego mind; it's fruitless.

Anyway, today my determination was very, very high. It had been like riding on the back of a Fireblade for 400 miles on a rocky road—uncomfortable and torturous at times, but you get there eventually. The energy of fear was just like a great big blob; I was covered in it, and I felt like I was fighting an enormous dragon, and the pain was coming and going like it was off the scale. But that's because I was learning to balance the energy. The whole experience is something I'll never forget. My whole nervous system was literally shot to bits. By the evening, I was calmer, and the pendulum was getting slower, and I hadn't tried to numb the pain apart from that I had a small gin, but years ago that would have been quite a few gins until I couldn't walk and smoking over twenty cigarettes while gambling my wages away while crying to Keane. Those just perpetuated the low mood, which used more energy trying not to show it, because I hated showing any signs of weakness. To be anything, we have to experience its contrast, so if showing a weakness was going to let me experience strength, then I was up for that. Massive fear would equal massive love. Anyway, now I was learning to observe those energies, no reaction to anything without thinking before responding, no flying off the handle, no extreme impulsive behaviour, and no disrespect to myself or others. It was getting easier, but the whole process was a painful one.

But I knew that when connected to God/source/soul/peace / the universe or whatever you want to call it, I felt peaceful, free, fantastic, healing, and I could feel it like something was healing, a bit like when you know a scab is healing. I was trying to stay there in that space. But it's just BEING; there shouldn't be trying. And that was my mistake over the years. The mind likes to mess everything up, and it'll fight you tooth and nail because it doesn't want to die or be integrated. The dark night of the soul is ego death, and it gets rid of a lot of shit so you're lighter when it comes to this bit. A spiritual awakening sounds like all light and roses, but I kept hearing, "Keep going," and I didn't have a choice. No one on earth would choose to do it. We only choose our path when we are soul. You only feel love as a soul, so the mere comprehension of how a human being with feelings actually feels is incomprehensible. But my God, we know about it when we get here. We are all being pushed towards ascension, whether we are aware of it or not, each at different levels, which is why we need more compassion, because whatever level you are now, you've been them all. It happens through so many ways: near death experience, twin flames, a significant traumatic event, or being so severely depressed that the only way is up. You've experienced the hell.

These past few weeks I'd been gifted with seeing things from higher perspectives, I felt physically sick and had to run to the bathroom. My own manipulation and coercion were mirrored back to me, and I obviously hadn't dealt with the trauma of it, even though again I thought I had. Yes, I was aware of it. Had I let it go and forgiven? Well, pretty much, and yes, quite a lot, but something still needed dealing with.

My trust with the universe was built over time, as I opened my heart. Things were revealed to me, building a stronger trust. In the beginning, it was just blind faith. Now everything was coming to light—and I mean everything. I was expecting my heart to hurt again, but instead I just felt peaceful, like a samadhi moment but longer. It wasn't blissful, but I knew I was on the right path, as in this moment I was anxiety free. It must have been all the meditation and karma clearing I'd done. I'd seen into the depths of my soul, and there was more to see than I ever would have thought. All those years of experiences were etched in my psyche—all my wrongdoings, yet all of my good things too. But they merged into one. I hoped to stay there as long as possible before the gut-wrenching anxiety returned. I could see how I could train it to stay, be the observer of my mind, and not let stories in that would perpetuate my pain. Staying in that state of peace was my priority, and it became the most important thing in my life. I had done energy work, releasing fear and pain, and had done for years, and then I got it. The whole process could have been a lot shorter had I not succumbed to addiction, which happened because I was frustrated at not seeing any results. I hadn't learned patience. I hadn't learnt to watch my mind and go with the flow of the universe. The necklace my SP bought me one Christmas is a compass with "faith hope and love" written on it, and when she gave it to me, she said it was so I didn't get lost again. I had left her all those years ago, running away from facing my own pain and into a pile of shit you called my life. Gambling, drinking, smoking to fill any voids, and I had become a recluse, and I was just in isolation. I honestly thought I was agoraphobic, but I now know that it wasn't that. I was exactly where I was supposed to be. During that time, I read book after book and listened to podcasts over and over in between my addictions and being incapacitated with emotional pain. I should have realized then how heavy I'd let everything get and how tired I was and how zapped of any energy or life force. Those years, I thought I was mentally ill, and I just wanted to become rich so that I could afford the best psychiatrist in the world, as I knew it was all just a big mess inside. Yet all I lacked was **SELF LOVE.** The total eclipse of my heart had made it very dark, and I draw people close to me and then push them away again, reinforcing my unworthiness. I know we all struggle; it's just to what extreme. All of our fears will manifest over and over until we heal them, and for all I kept wishing I had done it sooner. I had to trust in the universe that I was exactly where I needed to be right now in this moment. Even during the shitty bits, I knew I was there and that there was no way I could have learned all of those lessons in one go. It's true, I could have learned them sooner, but honestly sometimes we just can't see them. We have our eyes wide shut. It's quite a painful realization, but you can only accept where you are right now in this moment, which is here as a soul, and it's perfect.

Week 3

I realized that all my fears had manifested. Fear had to leave; I refuse to live in fear. Each time I had feared cheating, abandonment, you name it, it had manifested. My total lack of self-worth was shown to me quite spectacularly. But I knew I was on my way to becoming free. Had all the pain been worth it? I guess I'll be able to say soon enough. I was drying my wings as the butterfly who had just metamorphosed. The metamorphosis had been painful and a struggle, just like the real thing. I had now transcended the mind, so there was no more pain and struggle. I was really understanding this.

Everything was painful, and I'd rather have been in labour for two weeks or at least as long as I knew the end was on its way. The unbearable was becoming bearable as I moved consciousness, and at times I could feel like I was just my soul and not my body or my mind. Then I wanted to keep this up and never stop. At least I was now seeing results from my efforts. I didn't know how long my gestation period was, so to speak, cocooned and uncomfortable, feeling the pain of the lashes, but I intuitively knew I was coming out of this. That's what completely propelled me somewhere. It had to; what else could it do. I'd wanted to die on the spot from the pain—that unbearable anxiety trying to sneak back in. The start of a panic attack for me started in my throat, but I knew it was just fear, and I wasn't letting it in; it really was like a balancing act. My SP used to say, "Go big or go home," and I kept hearing it, and then I saw myself as my soul choosing my own destiny, which I had previously been a menace to, to which I said, "I want to go as high as I can." They said, "That will be very painful," and I said, "That's okay, there's nothing stronger than the power of love." It seemed there was no more information than that. I had heard this in a vision before, not the same but similar. But now I knew there was no power greater than love, unconditional love. Love for self. My heart was thawing.

Today it felt like I had done the two steps forward and one back again. Things were coming up from the past left, right, and centre, and I had been shown a lot. My behaviour over the years was nothing to be proud of, but also I was guided to forgive myself, as people cope the only way they know how until they find a new healthier way. I thought, "Well, you haven't bought any cigarettes, and you haven't hit the bottle or used any other coping mechanisms that were usually your go-to." So actually, I was doing okay, and even if I felt like shit in that moment, I was doing okay. During meditation, I didn't feel pain, because the soul doesn't feel pain; and I was hoping that if I continued, then eventually I'd become a light body where pain did not reside. We're all told not to cry, and I had all these stored emotions; they were just stuck, and every trigger was showing me them, but I didn't know at the time how to release them. The truth was, everyone in my reality was just me pushed out; they were my beliefs, my feelings, my traumas, and my stories just replaying over and over and over, and for all I had read about this, I didn't really understand it. But I did now; it was my own subconscious mind playing out. But that was what was going to set me free. I knew that if I loved, respected, and cared for myself, then that would be mirrored back, total acceptance of myself, both light and dark. Then I'd be free. People-pleasing and protecting other people's feelings was going to stop; I was just going to protect my own.

My dreams felt really real, and I woke up thinking, "Please just stop torturing me." One dream reminded me of when somebody told me I had been abused. This was similar, as I said to the person in the dream, "It's come from past trauma," and they said, "What trauma?" Sometimes we don't see our traumas. I knew that feeling, and how I try to numb the pain with addictions. I said I had been facing the pain and that I had screamed in the woods. I knew how raw and painful it was.

I remembered reading Louise Hay's books years ago, and she wrote about looking in the mirror saying, "I love you." I remember at the time thinking, "That's awful." But I tried it again, and ugh. But back then I didn't realize how important it was, and I didn't know. Loving ourselves, treating ourselves with kindness and respect and love and care. I just had to persevere; we are not pieces of shit, but we treat ourselves as such.

Tonight's meditation was like a mirror as I saw everything I'd ever done and said to my SP, and she had just mirrored it back. I knew fine well what I had done, albeit unconsciously. That perfect mirror, seen with such clarity. There was pain as I heard myself say, "Why don't you love me?" but I'd heard it from the child's perspective, a young child, and then again when I was a little older. I knew it was a sign of trauma. Dreams reveal a lot when we are open to them.

Week 4

In this morning's meditation, I could feel the energy of love and fear at the same time. It was a strange feeling, but energy can only be transformed, and there's a fine line between love and fear. It felt like friction, and I felt how this this dis-ease could manifest as a disease in my body. I knew I was near the tipping point, where only love exists. Love never dies, love never fails; love prevails. Love is all there is. So I knew that there was fear left, and it was manifesting physically as anxiety, and I had to transmute it. I had to let more love in. All of the shit I had been purging for months now … I did feel lighter and freer. There was still resistance, but I knew now, and I could move it—not that it was easy. Fear cannot exist harmoniously with love; it rubs it up the wrong way. Love is warm and fuzzy, and when fear comes near it, it upsets the equilibrium. But love is powerful—so much more powerful than anything. The love and fear battle had been a long one, and I realized I had chosen that. I had chosen fear on a lot of occasions because of the feeling of familiarity.

Our human bodies gain strength from these insights. We refuse to be attached, manipulated, or controlled. We are set free, but not without a struggle. To know love in human form, you must know extreme fear.

It was arduous as my father wound had come up again and I heard myself saying, "Why don't you love me?" while I was in labour, obviously in pain, when he went to the club for a drink. It wasn't the first time I felt like that. The club and alcohol came before us. I don't remember seeing him on an evening as a child. It felt like a clawing for love while saying, "Please don't leave me," and trying to hold it so tight it could hardly breathe. The trying to hold on all those years felt like trying to hold on to the wing of a Boeing 747 in flight. It was hard, and I never once thought about letting go and floating off, but now I did.

I remembered the dream I had of him when he died. I was sat next to him as he said "Sorry," and I said, "It's all okay."

It felt like a never-ending roller coaster again, so I just lay back and relaxed into it, I had more tears, and I was wondering how many more. It felt like I was releasing a lot more. I thought, "Surely there can't be much more." I felt like I was dying, but I just kept moving forward, doing breathing exercises, trying to stay calm. We lived on pizzas during this.

I could barely move, but I knew I had to eat because your body takes a battering when you punish it over and over. I haven't been loving to myself over the years, I had beaten myself black and blue over and over like a continuous fight with Tyson. No more. Not one second more would I beat myself up or talk to myself negatively. So, I could either muster up everything I had to love myself or I could stay in this dark, desperate space for the rest of my life, masking the pain with addictions and alcohol. I'd come too far now to mask anything with alcohol or addictions. I had already cut out alcohol, and at least I didn't beat myself up for not being perfect, but I applauded myself and was moving in the right direction. It was healing and was certainly not easy, but I knew intuitively that it was going to be over soon.

I'd said it before, but this was the day it really resonated with it like reading a book for the second time. I'd missed a very important part. Everything playing out in my reality was a reflection of my beliefs, my traumas, my wounds, and my vibration. It was never any good trying to just to raise my vibration if all that shit was still deep inside. We will never get anything any different. It wasn't my fault, but it was my responsibility to clean up that shit like Louise Hay says—clean up the rooms in the house internally. Anything happening in my reality was just reflecting my inner state. If I don't feel worthy, I will be shown that. If I think I will always come second, I will be shown that. If I've been abandoned and I fear it, I'll be abandoned again physically, mentally, and emotionally. If you want to be chosen, then you choose you. If you want to be respected, then you respect you. If you want to see love, then you be love. If you don't want to see trauma replayed, then deal with it. If you need to heal, then heal, but you must love yourself 100 per cent. You're not some piece of shit who continually gets treated like an underdog, and if you are being treated that way, you are treating yourself that way first. So choose self-respect, choose love, choose patience, choose humility and compassion, choose peace, choose you. You are the most important person in your life; you get to love yourself as you'd expect others to. That is one of your greatest gifts.

I mean, what a realization—realizing I could change internally, and externally things would change, I'd read all the books, and I didn't really put it into practice. I just kept reading and reading, but James Allen wrote as a man thinketh. I knew this conceptually, yet my mind was saying,

"You just need to read one more book and you'll have the answer." That was stopping me from seeing clearly, and my eyes were wide shut. You want to know why the narcissist enters your life; it's to show you that inner you—your deepest fears, the thoughts of yourself, your negative beliefs. If you keep repeating the old story, the same old record, over and over in your head, then that's what will manifest; it's universal law, the law of attraction. Even someone who loves you can only treat you the way you treat yourself. At this point, I was seeing things from a higher perspective, and I knew that you could read all the books on earth, but until you and your soul are ready, you won't move forward. You may have a little more wisdom, but it's just in your head; you haven't put it into practice yet. Each time I asked the universe what I needed to do next, I got the answer through things popping up on my YouTube, quotes, memes, synchronistic numbers, insights popping up in my head—so much that I felt as if I had psychosis. The narcissist will say, "I love you." What they really mean is "My soul came here to show you what you do not want, and you have to have the strength to see this." They have the role of reflecting your inner shit right back at you until you wake up and say, haven't I had enough of this pattern? Don't I deserve more? You have to get to a point where nothing ruffles your feathers. No fear—drop all fears and limiting beliefs. How do you do it? Well, you choose, and you believe. Can I choose me? Yes. Can I love me? Can I count on myself? Can I respect myself? Can I forgive myself? You have to say yes. But then you have to have faith and stand in that unshakable faith.

I was feeling a little bit better, especially after realizing I've been on this journey for about eighteen years. It was an eye-opener how I'd done the same thing over and over, expecting different results; how I'd repeated unwanted patterns; how I could now change things by not repeating the stories in my head. I hadn't been for a while; I had learned to pretty much transcend the mind. I was feeling more in my soul. I was edging my way forward and feeling into it, and I was even more determined now, like my hair was on fire. Even though I was in bed, knowing I needed to rest, as this had taken its toll on my physical and mental body, I was exhausted and felt like I was in recovery. A lot of samskaras had been let out through meditation, but the real work was with all those big emotions coming to the surface, and it wasn't pretty. How I knew I had to love myself unconditionally and forgive myself. It was becoming easier, and I did actually feel compassion towards myself for the things I've done. I was just trying to protect myself, and the paradox is that you just hurt yourself. Fearing everything, being too fat, being too thin, being too skinny, being too mouthy, being too happy, being too sad, being scared of everything, yet being scared of letting anyone know how you feel. We lose trust in ourselves, in our intuition, which we lose altogether because we're so disconnected from ourselves.

I was still healing. I knew there was no point in trying to hurry it. I just took each moment as it came. A lot of the time, I was out of my mind and my pain body, but then it kind of worked its way back, and boy I knew about it. I had to energetically just move back into peace in my heart. I was really starting to understand it was just a balancing act. We have to embody it.

There were still things coming to light, and I knew I needed to rest. I knew all the times I said, "Why can't you just love me," that I should have asked myself the same question. I saw a quote yesterday, and it said, "I never knew how much I needed to love myself until I started to." After staring into the depths of my soul, I started to love me. I could actually feel the little spark. I was able to look back and see my lessons in self-worth and love. If you abandon yourself, you will always be abandoned until you find the love from inside. I watched a series on Netflix, and it had a song called "Where Is Love?" from the musical *Oliver!*. It's not from skies above or underneath the willow tree, but from within. We've all wondered, "Where is love?" It's what we all strive for, hunt for, search high and low for. We've been duped, manipulated, lied to, betrayed, and cheated in the search for love. It's inside, yet we continue to hunt for it, fill in that void temporarily with things that don't even matter. We came from source, and we will go back to source. We can feel it if we connect to it. True intimacy—into me see. It's a deep search of the soul, seeing all your wrongdoings, traumas, mistakes, and limiting beliefs clearly and forgiving yourself and letting it all go. There's no room in love for jealousy, regret, hate, fear, lies, betrayals or anything low-vibe.

Today was just another series of letting go, this time of fear. I'd let go of so many things, trauma, and wounds, and I could feel the fear, and it felt like I needed an exorcist to get it out. It felt very strong, and I knew there was one force more powerful than fear. I'd been fighting all my life and hadn't realized, and yet here I was; it was right in front of me. I had to just love it anyway. I remembered King Kong fighting with Godzilla again, which is basically the soul versus fear. I knew he would win. Godzilla fought to the end, exhausted and drained, and after the long fight, enormous and powerful. But this time he looks at King Kong and retreats. He knows his time is up. There's nothing left to fight, because love will always win. That's where we have to be ready to fight with love, with grace, with patience, and with boundaries. Then fear cannot win. Releasing fear is not easy, and I could feel it around my heart, my solar plexus, on the lower half of my body. But King Kong had looked at Godzilla with no fear—a look that says, "No, you won't win, so don't waste your time." That tiny God spark in you rises up to burn that fear right out, igniting a strength in its place. It's all just energy.

Anyway, this was extreme. The mind had sneaked in, upsetting me again, and I kept saying, "I cannot tolerate this any fucking more." I'd done everything I could think of—breathing, meditation, guided inner child meditation, and releasing fears meditations—but here I was, fighting again with a heavy heart and a heavy solar plexus. There was a wound still lingering that I thought I'd dealt with, but nope, it was back. I briefly saw, in my insight, my brother being born, and I had a feeling of being pushed out. Lots of us will have a wound like this and then carry it through life. We replay it over and over. Something so simple could cause you problems all your life.

This morning, I had a "God please grant me grace" moment more than ever before. It was painful; I'm not gonna lie. Lying awake at 3:00 a.m. is one of the best times to connect to the universe. The mind was trying to run another one of its stories, but I'd already waved goodbye to Godzilla peacefully. I didn't have to kill Godzilla, although the fight at times felt like one would die. It was more about learning to live peacefully with the other.

It felt like my grace had been granted. I'd seen myself in the mirror last night and asked myself if I'd had enough yet. The answer was obviously yes, and it was like I was answering myself. And then I heard "Have you? Have you really had enough?" like, over and over, like it was goading me. I had, yes, and I knew I had, and if I thought I'd surrendered before, I hadn't, and I was just watching to see if I'd surrendered enough to not enter into the pain again. It actually felt more like a choice this time, so I must have been closer than I thought. I didn't have anxiety in my belly; I'd usually notice that and ask where it is, because it didn't feel normal to me, and it would come back with a vengeance, like the universe says here and gives you a double dose. I just observed it; I didn't label it good or bad. I'd learned that much. The music was helping calm my mind, and it was hard to stay calm. The high anxiety was extreme to the point I thought I'd burst. I knew I wasn't supposed to live like that. Over the years, I just accepted it and thought, "This is shit," but nothing seems to have got rid of it. The torturous mind only made things worse and worse. I had to trust in the universe at this point and every other point from now. It's a funny feeling when we accept that we aren't in control of anything. That's the meaning of "Let go let God." Total surrender. When the pain is too much to bear and you feel like you're going to die of pain any moment, there's not much else left to do. Things deplete your energy, and comparing yourself to others is a definite no-no in that respect. It also attracts a lot of third-party situations as well, which is what always happened to me, and if I didn't want that in my life, then I knew what to do—heal that wound. I knew it was a wound; I just didn't know where it originated from. But it didn't matter; I knew it would just heal naturally now. Even right in this, I could feel the fear of that wound coming up into my throat chakra like a panic attack, and I just observed that too. I've been healing over the years without realizing it. I'd learned just to observe my panic attacks years ago; I just didn't know why they were there.

Today I saw family dynamics clearly. Our relationships are nothing more than tools, people playing roles to heal the original wound. And the narcissists in my life gave me every opportunity, yet I failed to see. I could continue beating myself up for not seeing, but the new me said, "Well, you know now, and you'll trust your instincts from now on." Rome hadn't been built in a day; it had taken me eighteen years of constant books and searching for the truth, and it was inside me all along. Love doesn't hurt, and I could give it freely regardless of whether it was returned. I had been shown a lot of insights and perspectives, and I felt freer than I had for a long time.

Week 5

I woke up crying again at 4:40 in the morning. I just had to ride with it. Everything was coming out, then it seemed like a lot of stuff that had been buried just wanted to come out. I had a knot in my stomach that I'd woken up with. I was aware of my addiction part, and it was like it all became clear. I mean, you can get knitting as an addiction, but any addiction is an addiction, and we seek it to numb pain. Unfortunately, my addictions had been more harmful, but they are just there to show us when we've gone off the beaten track. I turned to my addictions when I felt I had no choice, but we always have a choice. This was the toughest and most brutal thing I've ever gone through. It was extremely tough to endure, but the only thing you've got is faith that you're gonna come out the other side. If I thought the last dark night of the soul was bad, this one was something else. The addiction stops you from facing the fear and moving through and is extremely hard to break. For years I found meditation and did it regularly, and it helped, but addiction is a powerful force that you have to overcome.

I saw the brightest purple colour last night in meditation. It reminded me of my daughter trying to say "purple" when she was two. I knew it meant something; it was my third eye. I'd stopped smoking and drinking in the house and had gamble limits on everything because even though I'd blocked my cards, I would still find a way; that's what addicts do in their desperation. But surrendering wasn't easy either. I decided I was going to love myself from the inside out. I could not fight any more. I was tired, but I will not be defeated. Life was just a big game. To love yourself, have compassion for yourself and treat yourself with kindness and not the harsh way you've always done is no easy feat. No one else was to blame; I was treated how I allowed people to treat me, and that realization was big. I'd read up on so many things over the years and now they were all coming together; the jigsaw was almost complete. I'd seen people who desperately didn't love themselves do things that kept them angry and unhappy; they were the people-pleasers, the empaths that couldn't bear to see others unhappy. I knew healing didn't happen overnight, but what mattered was that it had started; that was the main thing. If I had remotely thought of loving myself before, I would have felt massive resistance. You can tell by saying, "I love you," to yourself in the mirror how much work you've got to do. I realized it had been a gift—a sandpaper-wrapped gift. What better way to learn than to see reflections of yourself from different perspectives in different people: all the self-loathing, self-hatred, insecurities, and jealousy all mirrored right back. I'd have laughed if it wasn't so clever. In my meditation, I realized how I doubted my intuition so many times with "Ah, that can't be true, all doubt." I had started my book over a year ago, and I knew the ending hadn't happened yet, but I knew it would happen. So, from the perspective of when I first started the book to now has changed. There're bits at the beginning that can be picked out from when I doubted my own intuition. I felt like I'd been tossed into the mud blindfolded, naked, and bound; and just when I thought the pain was coming back, a feeling of peace came over me, and that was grace.

God wanted to experience himself in human form using the five senses, love in human form, yet what he sees is the opposite: the pain, the control, the greed, and the manipulation, which are all produced by the ego. There's just not enough love here. I asked myself what my experience on earth was; it was clear as day—fear everywhere. We have human love, which is riddled with fear and codependency. Basically, during a spiritual awakening we're pretty much squeezed through the wringer, showing us what love is not before we can truly experience love in its fullest truest form: love of ourselves, love for us, and compassion for what we've been through. We get to marvel at the love of self and wonder how we didn't feel it before. We were too hung up on our attachments or refusal to look at our pain, to really feel it and really let it go. To hold on tight to the breadcrumbs dropped to us over the years, holding on to the anxiety, wondering if we will lose whatever it is we thought we had. It's been a complete destruction of the self I thought I knew.

I realized I hadn't given much thought over the years as to why self-love was so important. I mean, did I really think I could just bumble around the earth, thinking I was worthless? Why hadn't I known this sooner? It's because we are in a state of amnesia and can only be awoken by severe pain and suffering. But to dream that there is something different—a freedom. We searched so hard outside of ourselves to find nothing but disappointment, betrayal, rejection, and so forth. I'd seen how people settle for their lot, thinking, "This is as happy as I'm gonna get." I think I'd woken up to a new me. I had a sort of love for myself. It was like I knew I was safe with me now. No anger, no negative feelings, but I was sure that there wasn't enough love in the world and perhaps not even enough love for myself. But that was going to change from inside during the last two years, when the concrete around my heart was being dismantled, leaving a big bright red mess that felt like it had been rubbed forever with a scouring pad. I was being bathed in a soft balm that was healing it, and that's all I cared about in that moment. That place I never thought I'd tread, but I saw myself on the podium, holding up my big, beautiful golden heart. And then I would have accomplished the most important thing in my life—that tipping point where fear would never be let in again. Was I sure? My mind wanted to argue about it, but my soul knew. It was a resounding yes.

Well today was rough, and I knew that addiction was just the body's way of trying to keep it safe from feeling the pain, but the only way was through, so I just had to keep on going. It was the worst, and I had a massive energy ball in my solar plexus to my heart chakra, and I mean it was heavy. I did some healing meditations and felt a slight relief, but this was years and years of built-up grief and trauma to let go of. I went for cigarettes, but I wasn't going to beat myself up for this perceived failure, because I didn't think I'd get through the night without any. I was really trying too hard, but this had to come out, and it was awful.

We get to look at ourselves. How we have allowed ourselves to be treated—to be manipulated, dominated, and controlled through fear. The other person with the narcissistic traits just teaches us to trust ourselves not to be gaslighted, to trust our intuition. All well and good when you're not awake, but there comes a point when we are awoken with a jolt and see everything for how it really is. For me, every single relationship I had was infused with my own unworthiness, my inability to speak and to feel my feelings, to have boundaries, and we end up feeling like we have "MUG" tattooed on our foreheads. Yet we repeatedly get treated like this and repeatedly ignore the signs and the red flags. I had allowed things to dictate the course of my life; I had closed my heart and become stubborn, prickly, and spiky, and pushed any feeling of anger down, resulting in passive-aggressiveness, and then wondered why the other person couldn't see how I felt. Yet I never expressed how I felt, due to insecurity and feeling vulnerable—that's the throat chakra closed off. Fear of losing the person if you speak up, fear of losing anything we are attached to, just constant fear, no peace. We cannot live in fear, and it's such a restricted and uncomfortable place to be. The truth is, you will be mirrored in each of your encounters. But that includes the good and the bad. It takes so long to recover from narcissistic abuse because, quite literally, they are mirroring all of your beliefs and self-worth back to you. We've abused ourselves by not trusting our intuition and having low self-worth, which is a perpetual cycle. Not one person with high self-worth would let another person treat them badly for any extended periods of time. I hadn't wanted to feel pain for obvious reasons. Who would? But this was the universe saying, "You've been stubborn enough now; you will feel the pain and release it." It was just so, so true.

I woke up feeling not as good as yesterday. I felt like I wanted to be sick and was gagging. I knew what I was going to go through, and I felt like I had the shakes. It was a fear of feeling the pain, and I have to be willing to go through the process that I had previously numbed out. I wasn't going to put that regret on the pile of unprocessed emotions. I just had to let it go now, and I could feel the anxiety churning inside, but it was smaller than before. It was enough, though, and it felt like whatever was coming was coming soon. Whatever was ready to come out was coming out regardless. I could feel it; it was like an energy, and this one was under my rib. I'd had this pain for twenty-five years, since my son was born. I thought it was where he had his feet, but now I knew it was just unresolved anger from that period. It just felt like it was round and dark and black with some spikes on it. It was palpable, like I could touch it. For something that had been buried for so long, it sure wanted to come out now. I could feel a pressure like a large needle that needed to pop it and let it down like a balloon. I could feel reflux, and the energy had moved into my heart chakra; I just had to close my eyes and let whatever it was move out. I was getting used to this process now. What seemed terrifying before felt necessary and kind of exciting, as the only focus was to feel better now. It was at times I felt like this that I would turn to addiction. If only I'd known how to let the emotions out, but scared of feeling the pain, I numbed it out immediately. I'd given up my impatience for this process, which seemed never-ending, I'd learned to just roll with it. Obviously, I wanted it to happen all at once, but I knew that that would be impossible;

it was a process. Over the years, I let things go slowly, which now seemed like a good thing, or this would have been even more painful. I could see the purpose of the dark nights of the soul preparing me for what was to come. I'd never learnt how to let my emotions flow or go, and maybe if I had, they wouldn't be spewing like Mount Etna right now. But I had a samadhi moment where I felt to be nothing and everything at the same time, like home where you always wanted to be, a peace that you cannot describe in words.

It's definitely a matrix; it's not real. I saw this last night. I'm still recovering from major nervous system damage, like I'm recalibrating and I can feel it. In my meditation, it was plain to see even as I'd reenacted my parents' actions from addiction to overprotectiveness.

Week 6

I said to my son, "Make sure you always let your emotions out, because if you don't, they'll come out like this." He said, "But I do, haven't you noticed?" He said, "You just keep them all in and pretend it doesn't hurt." Yes, I did, and I didn't realize anybody else had noticed. I was learning something different every day, and I think it was because I was taking more notice now. I realized that over the years I had shut down any feelings I had, and thought I was okay. I just popped them into a box, and then one day something triggers them, like a massive, massive pain, to release them. It's a gift, really, all the unwanted pain. They had taken me weeks, and I was still shaking this morning, and I could still feel the remnants of bits of stuck energy. I just felt like vomiting. It was like there was an exorcist clearing everything out. It had been very dense, and I did feel lighter even though I felt like shit. But I knew it was a process that I was going through, and this evening I felt much better. I didn't want to get too excited, and I knew more was on its way.

I felt really, really sick, gagging to the point of vomiting. I realized that even good people lie. It's not really them; it's just old stories playing out.

The universe got me a cat yesterday through a colleague at work. He's beautiful. He lost his owner before Christmas and needed a home. It took him five hours to come out, but trust had to be built.

I still felt like I needed to be sick. I honestly wondered how long this was gonna go on for. I had a bath with essential oils to relax and calm this nervous system down, and I wasn't beating myself up any more in my mind, which was good. The anxious feelings are still there, but I've calmed the most part down. There's still work to do, but I know I'm guided by my soul now. I only let the universe work through me. I'm still surrendering and just keeping at it. I didn't really know what proper relaxation was, but I sure as hell do now, and it doesn't involve alcohol, cigarettes, or gambling. I hadn't realized how much dark energy I'd stored as I lay in the bath remembering how I used to imagine letting all my worries float down the bath drain, but I must have given it up, thinking it was doing nothing, but it will have been doing something slowly. Nothing's really achieved with the click of a finger.

I knew the world was only as scary as I made it in my mind because the truth is there's only love here. I heard Eckhart say, "I cannot live with myself any more." Neither could I. Everyone at work was ringing in about anxiety, and I knew how they felt—like lava bubbling up inside their bodies, inside their abdomens, a tension so restricting and crippling. I had to keep surrendering more and more, and little by little it was leaving. So tense that it was painful to touch, all the muscles were so constricted that were once so painful I'd be bed-bound. It was six years today since I bumped into my SP, and I managed to re-enact all my old wounds. The cat was very affectionate, and I realized how I loved animals, but I'd never had one for a lot of years. I could see how the universe conspired by the way everything was happening. The moments of clarity were just glimpses of how I could eventually feel, and that gives you the strength just to carry on. I didn't have anxiety today or any pain, and I just kept saying to the universe, "Just let me in." I knew that my son was here for a reason; he was out of work right now, and I don't know what I would have done without him. We seem to be getting along better. We talked more, I understood him more, he didn't trigger me as much, if at all. In my meditation, I heard myself say, "That was rough," and I was crying, but it was like a cry of relief, like I knew things were going to get better, that things were going to be light and never be dark again. I knew I had stuff to let go of still, but I was feeling freer and didn't have the debilitating anxiety that plagued me 24-7. I remember thinking, "What the hell is all this about? Here on earth, all you see is pain, pain, and more pain." I thought, "I can't believe I've come here for this shit," but my soul was here to experience every emotion, like the soul's great big bucket list.

I was still removing the round, spiky red-hot lava-filled energy from under my rib. I knew exactly what it was. I still felt anger and bitterness even though I thought I'd forgiven, and it had been there all those years; it was only to see what I needed to work on and get rid of it once and for all.

I finally understood the stubborn wound, the one I tried to disperse with an imaginary hammer. But it was so solid it was like me hitting a great big rock. I knew this had been my thorn in my side; I was on my own during both my pregnancies, and then I realized seeing happy couples in pregnancy was a massive trigger for me. It was a massive wound and a half, and although I said I'd forgiven, I still had hold of anger, and I'd buried it. But burying it stuck to me like an energy ball growing bigger and bigger each time. Even saying, "I'm so angry," felt like I was being weak over being treated like that. It was unbelievable I couldn't see it, but I sat with the anger because I needed it to come out. I've done lots of processing today. I wasn't in a hurry any more. I had been a prude and had now just resigned myself to go with it, to just go with the flow. I was learning about myself, my shadow side. My SP told me not to speak to her again when I told her she was like her dad, but we were both like our dads, and it's not like they were bad people; they were just acting the only way they knew how.

Week 7

I had a meltdown at work. The trigger was a man who, no matter what I said, was not listening. It was just all the shit coming out, and it didn't have anywhere to hide at the moment. I can't run away from it, and it was just coming flooding out. I haven't felt like that to that extent before; it felt like everything that was frozen was now thawing, and I couldn't contain anything at that point; it just felt like I was recalibrating. It felt like all the tears I'd never cried were just wanting to fly out even at inopportune moments. The floodgates just opened with anger, sadness, and grief all in one. I was past the point most people would turn to medication to get rid of the feelings, and I just kept hearing "The only way is through." I knew this and had to keep going no matter what came up, and it was coming out like nothing I'd ever known, but it was a wound. I was not broken, and I was going to fix this like one of those vases they fill with gold in the cracks. Perfectly imperfect, yet whole and complete, I faced my shadow side, which had come up naturally at this point without me trying to find it, force it, or control it. I just had to go with the flow, and I was exactly where I needed to be.

Curing any addiction means you must transcend the mind; that's the only way; nothing else will work. I had that feeling again like I was half in, half out, and stuck in between love and fear, but I've done enough work to release so much fear that I was at the line, ready to cross. But there must be some stuck somewhere because I feared the thought of having to release something else again because it was so painful. More crying, more sadness, more grief, and my mind was saying, "You can't do it." Oh, but I could do it! The more conscious I was with my breath, the less I felt pain. It's simple, but it's not easy. By that point, that pain cycle was brutal, and you do not want to go there again at any cost, so you breathe, and you breathe consciously, and not only does the anxiety leave, but that physical pain leaves. Because I was fearing feeling the pain, it just made me breathe more and more and be in the present moment. It had taken practice, practice, practice to get to this point.

I was able to see how everything had shaped my thoughts and beliefs and how my self-esteem just kept dwindling over the years and the times I had struggled to get it back. It had been so long, and at times we feel so downtrodden we feel like giving up. I'd experienced all I wanted to on earth in that respect: the attachments, the codependency, that feeling of unworthiness that gnaws away at you at all levels. I was in touch with my soul now, and nothing was going to hurt me again. I was still healing from all my soul shocks and was starting to feel lighter. Well, let's face it; it couldn't have got any heavier, and it was just deciding itself when to let it out, which was a little disconcerting, but it was happening, and there was nothing I could do. We don't have control, and it doesn't belong here anyway, and that's the real meaning of "Let go and let God." I didn't want to be in the driver's seat anyway, because, let's face it, trying to control everything over the years was exhausting. Trying to bury all the crap with alcohol or gambling instead of facing it head-on was totally exhausting. No wonder I never had any energy. I could feel it coming back slowly but surely, back to the truth of who I really AM. The original soul shock of being born under this barren earth with all its conditions, control, and conformity. I was almost free. Without the severe emotional pain, I never would have got this far. Suffering is necessary until it isn't. I understood what had happened on the phone to that man, he was touching a raw nerve over and over and over again until it was intolerable. The aim was to have no more nerves to touch, and for all I thought, I had failed. It was the opposite and made me all the more determined to feel peace inside until nothing and no one could rock that boat. The power of presence is the only way with any addictions. Willpower will not work; the power of presence is the path of least resistance.

It came to me that I also had a brother wound. I'm not sure I liked it much when he was born, and I remember saying to my mum, "Why do you love him more than me?" The core wounds that were there weren't anybody's fault. Me and my brother used to fight even after I left home. We weren't really close, and the times I did spend with him, we still fought. But I do love him.

I was always trying to unlock the mysteries of the universe, trying to work it out like a puzzle, wondering what we were all here for, to believe in magic. But I never saw any at all. But looking back, I've had some amazing, wonderful, hilarious, happy, sad, indescribable moments, and I forgot. I cannot tell you what I've squeezed into my life.

The programme I watched told me I was dealing with a generational trauma; it had been diluted to some extent, but I was still feeling the full power of it inside my psyche and my DNA. Everything was starting to make sense at last: my insecurity of nakedness; the fear of standing naked in a crowd; and the woman in the programme with long hair, standing waiting to be executed. I felt it; like, I really knew how she felt. Not only that, she looked like we all looked like in my dream the other night when we were burnt and tortured and our hair was chopped off. I hoped that this was the last thing that was coming up to be healed. I thought I'd finished. I also realized that everything I disliked I had become.

I knew that if I didn't constantly become aware, then I'd get something else to push me further and that I'd held on to my anxiety for so long that it was like a part of me, but it wasn't. I know I could have chosen the path of least resistance and breathed it out, but I didn't. I had held on to it tight with constricted breathing and stomach muscles holding it tight in place. Fear on top of fear. Like, who would I be if I let it go? Anyway, I was realizing the truth as over the weeks I was shown more and more, and I'd even gone back to when I made my soul contract. I heard, "You will see love again in its purest form," and I said, "It seems like a very long time," and I saw my SP drawing of the butterfly that said "time flies" on it. A voice said, "You'll develop patience and forgiveness and become freer than ever before; you have to die before you die." I totally understood this, I'd listened to a lot of Wayne Dyer over the years, and I knew that the mind was connected with the heart like they understood each other.

Self-awareness is the cornerstone of emotional intelligence, and I read and learned about this, but it was never going to work, as I hadn't surrendered to the universe, and hence the addictions continued. For today I was free from those, and I didn't have that horrible pull any more. I still knew it was there, but I did not worry about having to take all my money out of the bank in case I did anything stupid with it, because I knew I wouldn't. That in itself was a feeling of freedom. There's still work to do, but I knew I was getting there, and that's all I ever wanted. There is a dimension of consciousness where you are not trapped on that level; it's a higher consciousness, an awareness.

All of our addictions start off so innocently, and before you know it, you're swept up into its unforgiving mouth and swallowed right up. They go to the ridiculously extreme, making sure we play the old wound of emotional abandonment but in another form.

It was like a puzzle today, but I was getting used to solving them. They were actually quite fun now. I was feeling a little bit better. I kept seeing the name Mary Magdalene, and Tina from school had also posted about her. And as I read the transcripts, I learned a little more.

I realized that the more I reacted to outside stuff, the more I suffered, then I just tried to let everything fly over my head—which, as we all know, is easier said than done. If you let it affect you for a period longer than necessary, then it grows and grows, and before you know it the energy has built up to attract more of the same but with an extra layer added on top. The energy literally expands with your attention, and like attracts like, so before you know it, you're dealing with something you really do not want. Yes, it's very hard to get into that space, but once you realize how important it is, you become aware of your thoughts because you do not want any more of that shit that you've already created. Not only that, but we are not just holding our own shit without letting it go, but everybody else is as well—all the shit that they projected onto us with their traumas, manipulations, and projections. So if you're an empath, you have other people's guilt and shame to deal with as well. It becomes so dense and heavy we can no longer live with ourselves, as Eckhart says, and we begin the slow process of letting it go.

Today again I was riddled with anxiety, but I was definitely learning to balance it, as hard as it was. I kept muttering, "Fuck you," under my breath, as it wasn't going to beat me, because I was stronger than it. I thought I'd mastered my wounds years ago, but what I'd actually done was bury half of it. So, I noticed there were dregs of that to clean up. All of a sudden, I seemed angry about a lot of stuff—things that I had tucked away, not wanting to look at. But as I sighed, "Just bring it on then," I waited to see if I was going to regret that, but at this point I didn't actually care. Again I felt I needed an exorcist to get rid of it; it was right in my solar plexus, big and spiky. I didn't really want to see it, so I closed my eyes and prayed that whatever it was would be healed in my dreams, because to be honest, I don't think my heart could have taken any more pain. I just wanted it to leave.

Week 8

Layer after layer after layer. I was quite sick of it now, even though I felt lighter and I could feel it getting better. I still needed to balance my energy, so no focus was going anywhere other than myself. It was torturous. The addictive energy had to be no more, which only happens with total presence, and that is tough, like a great big, long arduous fight. But I had endured this for a long time, and it felt like a massive punishment, but I knew it was pushing me into presence, into total surrender. I was waving my white flag now. I listened to Eckhart. He popped up, and it was called "Dissolving the Pain Body," and I knew that was exactly what needed to be done. I told my inner child, "You can just let go now."

Tolle said that the pain is the fuel for awakening. Oh yes, it certainly is! It leaves you with nowhere to go, nowhere to hide. No addictions or obsessive behaviours work any more, and then you are left standing, begging it to stop, doing breathwork, and trying to stay connected as I had practised. But my God it was tough. Yet I could still see a light at the end of the tunnel, and it was bigger than when I first started, at which point it was pitch black. I guess it just builds, it gets better, and you become more positive, and you develop more faith. And as much as the pain was still there, I could feel the other side slowly but surely, and it seemed like as my trust grew, my pain was leaving.

Being a GP receptionist isn't easy, but for twenty years I've been there, and I've seen people in anger, desperation, severe selfishness, pettiness, confusion, rudeness, kindness, and love. I've seen the whole spectrum. But I learned a lot of lessons there. People tend not to self-help or self-heal; I don't think they know how, or they don't want to. Some expect a magic pill, and they want it now. Some like to label themselves, diagnose themselves, call the GP wrong, not realizing we are all human, the negativity invading every part of their lives. The complaints I found quite ridiculous. I knew we weren't supposed to live like this—people desperate for help just to feel better, not realizing their own power. For me, I was still learning to release and let go, and for someone who would hide their feelings and only ever looked happy for the most part, I felt quite lucky. Every single one of us has emotional pain stored, causing havoc inside our bodies and affecting our minds, our weight, our hormones, our mental health. I struggled with mine for years, but I was an avid reader, so I have gained a lot of knowledge on how the mind works and affects us in negative ways. It wasn't all for nothing, and I felt relief from knowing that. The overly compassionate health professional can be walked all over and treated similar to someone in an abusive relationship. I lacked assertiveness when I started the job, and I still had right up until recently, and the reason being is we think that we're all the same with the same hearts. We're not. The zero-tolerance policy of abuse proves it. Who would have thought that GPs or any emergency staff would be abused. Anyway, today I realized that my inner wounds were mirrored right back at me, and I'd never have known, no matter how deep I dug, what they were, but silence had spoken. I had my own control issues, which had led me into relationships with control issues. But when you're in a lot of pain, any control you try to have just slips through your fingers. That's what happens with control; the universe has a way of showing you that you have absolutely none. The meaning of "Let go let God"

God Knows

had more meaning now than ever. I wasn't scared of being on my own; I wasn't scared of dying, because I knew we never really did. I didn't need codependent relationships—or any relationship, for that matter. I found that my triggers seemed to melt away the more I was aware of them. Over the years, I just swapped one addiction for another, and that didn't work either. How funny: looking back trying to maintain the status quo, which was never going to dissipate until I completely surrendered, I muttered, "Fuck you," again under my breath before I set about releasing this little bastard once and for all. I spent all those years not feeling anything, to have and to feel it all at once—and I was even angry at that. In fact, right now I was just one great big angry ball of fire—a painful angry ball. But also with a big, massive relief that I knew I could heal it, even as they went deeper and deeper and deeper.

The karmic stories had well and truly played out, and I was well aware of how I'd ended up in some of the situations I'd been in. My eyes had been tightly closed. No one likes to see anything that's going to hurt them.

Most of my partners had been heavy drinkers, apart from my SP. But that was another thing I had to heal. My dad was a heavy drinker. I'd become a heavy drinker. I saw dynamics in other relationships. If you were treated as a puppet on a string as a child, you will end up in a relationship being a puppet on a string; if you walked on eggshells, you will end up in a relationship walking on eggshells. If you had a possessive parent, you'll end up in a relationship with a possessive partner. If you had a protective parent, you'll end up in a relationship being protected. If you had a perfectionist parent, you'll end up in a relationship with a perfectionist. Not just a romantic relationship, but any relationship will show you this. We're also attracted to these by familiarity. I even wrote that I felt like I had the Stockholm syndrome. The colour seems to drain from your life the more darkness gets in. But those colours were coming back.

We hear that the truth is within and that everything we need is inside of ourselves, but we never really understand it and wonder where it is. It's buried, that's where it is. It is just covered in a whole lot of shit. We've been like shit magnets all our lives and are now frantically trying to get rid of it. It feels like quicksand. I always wondered where my fear of quicksand came from, seeing as I'd never even seen any before. But it's the same bogged-down feeling or the drowning feeling we all dread. I used to have dreams of quicksand. And then you discover that even that bogged-down feeling had been-bogged down. Suffocated. We release it all the only way we can when we're not aware in the form of disease and decay and mental health issues. But in silence and presence, we slowly emerge. I lay listening to the birds at five this morning and thought I'd heard them before, but this time I really heard them; like, I could hear six or seven birds singing at the same time clearly, and it was like magic. That's what being present is. This was yet another positive turning point for me, as so much more was revealed, and I can't even explain it. The truth will be revealed to you, but it can never be explained. My truth will be different to yours because we've had different experiences. Doubt had been my biggest enemy; it had dampened and hidden the truth. I'd picked my own lessons before I came for my path here, and I dismissed them with my ego mind and didn't use my intuition. But to be honest, putting them all together, they were unmistakable. And then I thought, "It's just so obvious," now that they were the signs I would actually pick if I had to choose them now. It's something you can't quite explain in words. Being shown my dark and my light sides. I was everything, everyone, and nothing all at the same time, and it was unbelievable. The power of love over the power of doubt was far more supreme.

Week 9

I didn't know whether to laugh or cry as my solar plexus chakra appeared to be next. I'd only just recovered from the sacral chakra. I had a look, and it was releasing shame and all the things we judge ourselves harshly for. Yes, I got this. I had beaten myself black and blue. I knew I didn't want the pain, so I had to let go of it; it was as simple as that. I laughed as I said it was simple. But this one was actually simpler. I knew this. I'm human; I make mistakes like everybody else. The only difference was I didn't learn from mine very quickly; I went back to them over and over again, just looping and replaying them over.

It was a funny way because I had more and more clarity. Yesterday I knew that all the years of chronic anxiety and panic attacks were just a taster of the unbearable pain you get to go through going through that dark forest, and it's so unbearable that you have no choice than to go within and be still, pray it stops, and trust in the power of love. The scary moments were just a taster of the healing you need to do and the feeling you'll have as you come back home. The more anxiety you have, the more it pushes you into love. It has to be this way. I got that now. I had a vision of being in a thumbscrew and someone asking me who would win, the heart or the head. Like, it's in the heart. The heart will win over and over; that means no fear, just free, just being home, where you belong. I never really felt at home, but from now on I would always choose love over fear. Fear will fight you, always and fiercely, but you have to come this far. Keep fucking going. It's like the man digging, and he's just about to reach the goal but gives up and turns around, but one more strike and he would have hit gold. It felt like the light was getting bigger, and I knew the April full moon had been powerful. I dismissed all that as rubbish, but now I knew it. I'd let the cat out when I was terrified he'd run off, but he scaled the fence and went for a wander for four hours. Two nights later, I knew I had to face the fear and open the door again. If you love something, set it free. He came back quickly, and I lost the fear. He never went far. But there was more to overcome. That was a small test.

By now I was really angry, and I was finding it hard to choose love over fear, but my God, was I paying for it. It was anxiety on steroids, but it just felt natural to me now as I just breathed in love and breathed out fear. I was getting better at this, trusting myself, my own intuition. I could still let people drain me and get annoyed with them for letting it happen, and I also hated seeing it happening to others.

I knew I'd never been good at relaxing, but I had been doing it. But it felt forced. Now it was more natural. My nervous system was shot to pieces, as I had internalized everything throughout my life and it was full of shit basically. The panic attacks were just it wanting to come out, and the natural thing to do was to bury it with addictions. We do anything to stop it but relax and breathe, and I was angry at myself for half-realizing this but taking no notice. Yet I was grateful that I knew it now. I had indeed surrendered, as I couldn't tolerate it any more. I had had little or no faith in myself, no love for myself, no forgiveness for myself, and I beat myself black and blue. And it was like attracts like; that's exactly what I got. The chaotic feeling of an addiction is exactly why it's an addiction; I just hadn't figured that out. You are addicted to chaos and pain and that's what the nervous system feeds on until you calm it down and stop filling it with crap. It doesn't like it because it doesn't like change and it takes time, and I realized this. And the body takes time to change to your new state, no matter how small the change. It's painful both physically and mentally. It had been a little while since I cried, considering it was nonstop at one point, but today I did. Fear and ego were dissolving, which was just perfect.

My parents were born in the years of fear, as a lot of them were when the wars were ending. I wondered why I'd had the experiences I'd had, and it was to annihilate fear and anxiety. I felt like I'd been carrying everyone's; it was so heavy. I dropped some, but there was still some lodged, and I was digging deep to find it. I wanted it out; what was once bearable no longer was. Breathing exercises helped as long as I could focus continuously on them and not let the mind swoop in and ruin it. Cleanliness is next to godliness, and I realized that this was inside—as in spiritual purity, not personal hygiene. I just wanted to clean my mind and have a free and peaceful mind, and I was going to get it. I was physically sick as I realized I'd held on tight to all my abusers, expecting them to change and just giving, giving, giving, I was a fixer, yet the only person I needed to fix was myself. My solar plexus seemed to burn, and it was painful but necessary, and it was cleaning it out, and I knew it was coming because I could feel it. I knew I'd feel it today because it was my dad's birthday, and he was with me. I cried a little as the solar plexus is the "shoulda, woulda, coulda" chakra, and I knew I couldn't have done any different with what I knew at the time. I could wish I'd known this when I was twenty or whenever, but I didn't, and I couldn't beat myself up again for not knowing. I truly forgave myself and everyone else this morning. I had pain in my heart. I think all negative energy was burning away to get to it. I didn't care how much it hurt, because I knew it would be worth it. While in the fear, I stood outside and I felt the fresh air, and it felt like freedom to me.

Who'd have thought that we could have so many demons. I'd obviously asked to experience a few while I was here, but the underlying vibration was always love. I had body issues; hang-ups; addictions to numerous things; extremely bad relationships with violence, chronic anxiety, and pain. I'd been gaslighted and manipulated. I had trust issues, lack of self-worth, and love, and I'd suffered narcissistic abuse and had my own narcissistic traits, anger issues, and jealousy. I was doubtful and was working from my wounded feminine energy. But I had faced and healed so many of these, and all of the ego deaths and dark nights of the soul served to crack my heart open. And you find that a heart attack was just the heart saying, "Okay, I've had enough of all this darkness and ego shit, and I'm going to scream out at you painfully. I'm buried in all this shit, and I cannot breathe, so what else am I supposed to do?" The wounded heart, drenched in pain, trying to bandage it with alcohol and addiction so as not to feel, and I knew it was all backwards. I was feeling a lot lighter, and it had really been so painful. I could breathe. I saw my bracelet, and it said "Sometimes you've gotta fall before you can fly," and I knew this to be true. I had always dismissed a lot of things—including loving myself, not realizing it was literally the most important thing. I had already cried over the things I had done to myself, wondered how or why I'd ever treat myself in such a way when I wouldn't even have treated an enemy like that. I lacked divine feminine energy, and I was going to get it back. I was going to be strong, be loving, be kind, be intuitive, trust myself, and love myself beyond anything. And I see so many of us treat in ourselves badly, and I will do anything and everything within my power to drag us all up, kicking and screaming, to love ourselves more, to treat ourselves better, to eliminate addiction, to eliminate unworthiness and self-berating, to uncover our sacred hearts again that have been buried under lifetimes of shitty mind and ego mentality. I'm returning to love. I'm glad I got to experience the other side now, because to know what you do want, you must experience its opposite. That's duality. It's law. The apple doesn't go up without coming down. And now I was certain as to what I wanted, and to love me was enough in my perfect imperfection.

Week 10

This one was really hitting me where it hurts, which was everywhere. Like walking on hot coals while on fire, I couldn't tolerate it a moment longer. It seemed relentless, and I knew I either crossed over to the bridge by breathwork or I could stay stuck here in purgatory. During meditation, I was shown some of my past thoughts. They were dark, and I realized how I had closed my heart and that any dark thoughts had caused my anxiety bag to get fuller and fuller, along with its regret, anger, rage, guilt, and unforgiveness for any other negative thing you picked up along the way.

I was now off work with this never-ending anxiety. It's funny, as it was in my solar plexus, and that's where shame lives if it's not released. It's painful. I had shame of being weak or not expressing my feelings and not saying I'm not okay. How ironic.

I was squeezing through this and pushing on through. I still felt like I'd been kicked all over but kind of relieved. I didn't feel like I was holding on to the electric fence with a very high voltage; it was painful. Things were coming up to be released—things I didn't even know I had. But they made sense. A lot of things made sense now. It was deeply personal, and I can't believe I didn't see it. But honestly, I forgive. I released myself from that pain and anybody else involved. I saw a glimpse of the inner peace again, but I had faith that one day it would be here to stay. I knew I'd created my life before I came, and it was all written in the stars. And I was now regaining my strength, and I was going to only cocreate wonderful things from now on.

I was slightly better than yesterday; I was relaxing. I could hear all my bad thoughts and beliefs over the years that manifested one way or another, either by pain or in my reality. Physically, I'd come out kind of unscathed. I saw people in agony day in and day out. I mean, I did have negative energy stored as pain under my rib, and low back pain, which is classic. It's the root chakra that's unbalanced. Mine had manifested as more mental pain, a real unseen pain. I was going through this immeasurable pain so much that I was incapacitated at points, but I knew it was nearly over as I heard it's darkest before dawn.

The pain was healing me paradoxically. I felt like I was trying to get a square peg into a round hole, but I was getting through it. The feminine energy was not weak, but we had all become small and weak, weakened by fear and threats, and had lost our power to toxic masculinity, which has no place in my world ever again. I felt I hadn't fought enough, but I had with what I knew at the time, as I only saw the good in everybody. But now I knew better. I knew my weak boundaries had played a big part in how I was treated, and to blame others was now ludicrous. I was to become a rising phoenix who tolerated no more shit. She found her self-worth and self-love, she who knew she deserved love despite her mistreatment over this and past lives. I was not a victim but a conqueror, an absolute goddess, and nothing and no one was going to keep me down. I could feel a strength rising within me, and I wasn't letting go again. I will be free. I wondered if I could ask the universe to take more pain in a shorter space of time, but to be honest, the intense pain was enough, and I think it was to the max already. Through that pain, I could again see the puzzle clearly: the whys, the hows, the should'ves, the could'ves. There was a clarity, and I knew that if I had any doubts or needed answers, I just needed to ask and I'd get them. Who'd have thought it? The light was at the end of the tunnel, but it was bigger and brighter, and I knew I was gonna bask in it when I was right in the light, until I actually was the light. That goal was ever clearer.

I started my book to make sense of everything, and I could see the progress over the years. I could see that, unfortunately, we have to endure some narcissistic abuse so that we learn the lessons of trust in our own intuition. They give us clear red flags in the beginning. It's up to us if we choose to ignore them. You have to have compassion, forgiveness, empathy because hurt people hurt people, and if you do the opposite, it will only perpetuate the cycle. Anger was prominent in my family line. I'd had two broken noses and seen two family members break their hands in anger, and that was only what I had seen. I thought I'd dealt with my anger years ago, but I had only internalized it instead of acting it out.

Working all week and ascending was tough, obviously. I was off work because there was only one focus at the moment, and that was to stop the pain—actually not stop it, but release it. Just because something was introduced in 1926 by Henry Ford—the eight-hour, five-day week—does not mean it's sustainable now, and I decided I was going to find my creativity and BE more in my free time. We've all been programmed to accept this as normal, but quite frankly you can't pour from an empty cup. We actually do get what we think we're worth; it's the same as when you go for unavailable people. Deep down, we don't think we are worth more, and this is lack mentality. And this was something I was also going to release.

I knew when this hit me that I was going to have to slay it like a big dragon. It felt like breathing its hot fire in my belly like torture, making me want to reach for anything and everything, and I knew I had to feel its pain to taste the sweet, and it was like torture with tiny bits of grace in between, because if those weren't there, you wouldn't be compelled to carry on. I said the serenity prayer in my head over and over, and I was tired like I'd slain it physically. Releasing fear, deep regret, guilt, grief and shame all in one go was extremely taxing and painful, and it took me to its very depths, and there was no more being able to push it down. All the pushing it down to deal with later on was forced upon me like a tidal wave, like a tsunami, and there was no stopping it. Faith keeps you going, then you know you're gonna come out better on the other side. It was like my last nerve had been exposed—swollen, red, raw, and ready to be healed. I didn't know how, apart from being in the present moment, which I had practised, and this was the biggest test. I also knew the only way was to balance the energy by heart and mind coherence. Stop the swinging pendulum. And I knew I could do it. It was once far more chaotic than this, swinging fully from side to side. Now it was just bobbing really slowly from side to side, but I was going to make it still. My karmic partners over the years had taught me lessons I never really knew until now. It was perfect—painfully perfect.

My solar plexus healing had coincided with the solar flares, and I realized that everything that had been too painful to talk about was just coming up and up and up; then it had to be healed. That feeling of despair was not sustainable, and I would never take my own life, but it would be unbearable, so there was no choice. Fight on. And yes, the fight was on fully. I will not be defeated. I said it before, and I meant it. The leopard programme showed me the strength through desperation, fighting to stay alive one way or the other. Someone once told me only the strong survive, and "Who dares wins" was the motto of the SAS, which was something the universe was communicating to me cryptically with a memory I had. I took that as a sign, as I had then. I could see clearly how the clues came up over the years. I knew it then, but my mind made me doubt it, as I'd lost my intuition. But now I was 100 per cent certain as to what was happening. My solar plexus was the last one to heal until my heart chakra. "It's darkest before dawn" was very apt, as it was the most excruciating pain. It felt like a burning sun was inside my body, with the feeling of an itch. But that only made me know fine well it was healing.

Week 11

There was nothing quite like the sheer agony to make me determined, and I just kept saying over and over that only love was real. Fear cannot exist where love is. I knew it was the answer just to keep loving me and put love where the pain was. It was extremely difficult to balance my energy to that extent. Hence the previous dark nights of the soul that took the ego away in little bits so that I at least had half a chance of the mind not getting in the way. But oh my God I knew about it until "God have mercy on me" came out of my mouth. I had to have faith that it was coming, and I was in no doubt that I had to trust the universe like I had never trusted it before.

Well, grace had been granted for now. I didn't have the pain. I felt like I was burning from the inside out. I want to crawl out of my own skin today. However, I was now aware that I couldn't have done it myself; the universe had carried me through with faith.

I realized I was the only one causing this pain. I had chosen it; I'd held on to it for dear life. The times I wasn't in pain, I was present, staying out of my mind and any stories and fears it wanted to try and sneak in. Now it was time for a real change. There was a spark inside of me now that was ignited and was never going to go out. I still felt tearful, like I could cry at the drop of a hat, but what was the point in that? it would now just produce more sadness perpetually. Time to drop the victim mindset. I could continue to torture myself or not. Simple. Not easy, but simple. Unbelievable, but pain is necessary until it isn't. My consciousness has increased, so I was more aware of my thoughts and didn't let the thoughts ruin my vibration, therefore feeling better and better, and I knew it was all going to be worth it.

I now realize the importance of self-love to a larger extent. The push of the self-hatred and the pull of self-love cause symptoms akin to mental health illness—just trauma, guilt, and shame all perpetuated by replaying our thoughts and stories that we go over in our heads, reinforcing our own worthiness with our own negative self-thoughts and self-talk, tested by other souls who came here to show us where we were missing the mark, testing us to see what we'd put up with in the name of love. Again, this is trying to force a square peg in a round hole. A balancing takes place as we come out of the dark night of the soul, the painful ego death that strips us bare and removes anything we no longer need and that no longer serves us: our limiting self-beliefs,, the stories we've told ourselves, the blame and shame we've somehow riddled ourselves with so we can barely see the real us. This is what it means to become whole and free—unburdening ourselves of all the stuff that no longer serves us. I could smell that freedom. I could feel it. Now it was time to fully embody it. To love myself like never, ever before and like I never thought was possible. All my lessons were plain to see: no blame, no shame, just love. And that's enlightenment.

I know I create my reality now 100 per cent. I'm creating all wonderful things from now on. My self-worth and self-love have multiplied. I'm grateful for the experiences I've had—something I never thought I'd say. But now I will focus on regaining my strength and power back. I'm finding it hard to believe I had lost them. How the darkness tried to infiltrate the light. My light.

Along the way, I was gifted with people in circumstances to help me grow, to show me where I needed to heal. All things came at the right time; the trying to break me did not work. Yes, I'd put up with more crap than I needed to, but I learned a valuable lesson. We really are more powerful than we imagine.

The "Why don't you love me?" question reared its ugly head again as I heard a baby cry next door. I thought I'd dealt with this one, but the straggly bits were still there, and it needed dealing with just when I thought it was over. But I could tell it nearly was. Yes, I felt alone while I was pregnant, and I caused myself stress and guilt after that, my baby coming early, and then leaving him some nights in hospital to go home to sleep because I was so exhausted. I hadn't really stopped to see how I felt, and just stuffed it down and bottled it up. My dad was ill at the time we met Jan. I barely saw David, and then he didn't see his son until he was two weeks old. I was real angry, and I'd never let it go. That was twenty-five years ago. It's a long time to hold on. Even that twenty-five-year-old inner child needed a hug, and she's going to be fine now.

I knew it had to be a place where love overrides fear and doubt. It's just a mindset, not wanting to get hurt easily after the continuous chipping away of the self-esteem. Even our most loved ones test us. No enabling, just total tough love, or we don't grow—and they don't grow either. We've got to get to a point of complete authenticity, resilience, and faith. Nothing more and nothing less. This is where I was headed, and no one or nothing was going to get in my way. That no-fear mindset creates inner peace eventually after the fight. But in the midst of it, you surrender, and that is the secret. It's an acceptance of all of you: the good, the bad, and the ugly. There's no snowflake behaviour—an inner strength you never thought you had. This is your dance space, and nobody puts Baby in the corner. You chop wood and carry water. I never understood that saying, but we take responsibility, and we fight for ourselves. Well, there's no warmth and no fire and nothing to drink without that. We realize our traumas are gone; we only have here and now and that we are all safe now. The inner child with that feeling of dread, abandonment, and rejection will come up to be healed, and the one who just triggered you will be a loved one who loves you enough to (unconsciously) trigger that in you to be brought into the light and healed. All of our fears and traumas will be mirrored back to us until we finally fight to become free. The wishy-washy attempts are no more. There's a fire in your belly that isn't going to go out ever again. You will not be defeated no matter what, and that's where you'll find yourself when you have had enough of the pain. Freedom. Total freedom and love of self, which is beautifully perfect. Who could love you more after everything you've been through. That love stands the test of time, and nothing and no one can take it away. You can never fear it being swept from under your feet. Absolutely solid. Your inner strength has come through for you. You have come through for you!

Afterword

All truths are true if you believe them to be so. If I think I'm worthless, others will too, and they will treat me accordingly. But if I have self-worth, I also get treated accordingly. Looking back, I see that I continued to live in the past with my thoughts, my regrets, my conditioning, and my traumas. That's why we need *now*. There's nothing more to add than that, as it is the truth. We are what we think we are—magnificent creators of the universe. I am not going to be creating misery any more, and that's true freedom. As I've said before, the truth will set you free. The truths I thought along the way were never the truth. My beliefs were distorted truths. Only love is real.

Milton Keynes UK
Ingram Content Group UK Ltd.
UKHW031118081124
450926UK00001B/173